GOD *beyond* GENDER

GOD *beyond* GENDER
FEMINIST CHRISTIAN GOD-LANGUAGE

Gail Ramshaw

FORTRESS PRESS   Minneapolis

GOD BEYOND GENDER
Feminist Christian God-Language

Scripture quotations unless otherwise noted are from the New Revised Standard Version Bible, copyright © 1989 by the Division of Christian Education of the National Council of the Churches of Christ in the United States.

Interior design: Peregrine Graphics Services
Cover design: Patricia Boman
Cover art: Sonia Terk Delaunay, Electric Prisms, used by permission of Musée National d'Art Moderne, Centre Georges Pompidou, Paris.

Library of Congress Cataloging-in-Publication Data
Ramshaw, Gail, 1947-
    God beyond gender : feminist Christian God-language / Gail
Ramshaw.
      p.   cm.
    Includes bibliographical references and index.
    ISBN 0-8006-2774-1 (alk. paper)
    1. Sexism in liturgical language.   2. God—Name.   3. Feminist
theology.   I. Title.
BV178.R355   1995
264'.0014—dc20   94-17695
                                                    CIP

The paper used in this publication meets the minimum requirements of American National Standard for Information Sciences—Permanence of Paper for Printed Library Materials, ANSI Z329.48-1984.   ∞™

Manufactured in the U.S.A.   AF 1-2774

99   2   3   4   5   6   7   8   9   10

CONTENTS

67 - 74

v

PREFACE

During the years of my youth, most Christians in the United States replaced the archaic Latin or Jacobean English of their public worship with some form of the American vernacular, thereby delighting some of the faithful and horrifying others. But Christian linguistic reform is never completed. The comparatively rapid changes in American English reducing androcentric bias and the continuing analysis of the effect of androcentric speech on the personal and public psyche have challenged not only the secular culture but also the church. The current wave of Christian linguistic reform, producing once more both delight and horror, seeks to diminish, if not totally eliminate, androcentric speech from the language of worship. In this book I am concerned with the most tumultuous aspect of this pursuit: the reform of God-language in the liturgy.

To undertake writing about this complex and controverted issue, an author is likely to have had varied experiences in the church: some positive, to inspire energy for liturgical renewal; and others negative, since it is difficult for people who are innocent of the crisis of feminist awareness to take these controversies seriously. I am one such person, paradoxically richly nurtured by a church that constrained me. One professor, after four years of teaching me the theology of Christian worship, advised me that I had no future in the field because I am female. Clearly, I heeded his teachings but not his advice. I keep listening to both extremes of the conversation, and I have changed my mind on several significant issues in the last few years. I remain grounded in the actual weekly worship of the people of God. Separatist worshiping groups have their own value and offer a unique contribution to this discussion, but as a feminist Christian parent who sits with her daughters in typical parishes on Sunday morning, I urgently feel the pastoral need to reform the official books of the churches.

I am also a Lutheran. Lutheran liturgical tradition offers a model for contemporary worship reform, which I seek to follow in this book. The process is: (1) Examine the actual lived experience of the church. (2) Analyze how liturgical structures and speech form the minds and ethics of the faithful. (3) Study the Bible and the Christian tradition to discover the most effective presentation of the gospel in the past. (4) Edit out what obscures the Spirit, what no longer, to use Martin Luther's phrase, "speaks the gospel." (5) Reinterpret what is salvageable so that it more clearly "shows forth Christ," to cite Luther again. (6) Make necessary adaptations and write new material in the vernacular, in order that the assembled community express not the status quo but the astounding mercy of God. The issue is much deeper than determining which words are in the Bible, for Luther was no fundamentalist. Rather, Luther taught the faithful to examine each biblical book for how useful it might be in conveying the gospel. Some biblical words brilliantly show forth the Word, but others, Luther contended, did less well or quite poorly at this central task. Luther urged the faithful to find the words that best reveal the Word.

I have been assisted in my study by many people. I thank all the women who share my inquiry: the conservative women grounded in the old speech, my students at La Salle University writing papers about God, the post-Christian feminists finding truthful words only outside the church. Most especially I thank my sister Elaine J. Ramshaw and other feminist Christian scholars who are laboring to lay the pavement for a new path. I thank my colleagues, both women and men, in the North American Academy of Liturgy, for their continuing efforts in this task. For a decade I have been trying out my ideas in scholarly essays, mystagogy, liturgical texts, and lectionary resources. I thank my editors who willingly offered this laywoman a megaphone: the late Howard Galley of Seabury Press; Gabe Huck of Liturgy Training Publications; Bernard Benziger of Pueblo Publishing Company; Michael Naughton, O.S.B., of The Liturgical Press; Kevin Seasoltz, O.S.B., of *Worship*; Virgil Funk of Pastoral Press; Karen Ward of *Worship '93*; and Timothy Staveteig. Finally, accompanying me throughout has been Gordon Lathrop, *sine quo fere nihil*: to whom my gratitude.

one

FEMINIST CHRISTIAN GOD-LANGUAGE AS DOXOLOGICAL

Religion includes distinct though interrelated categories of language. One category, the speech of primary religious experience, narrates a vision or describes the images of private reverie. Another category, the language of theological reflection, articulates a precise formulation of either the individual believer or the ecclesial body. Different as these types of religious speech may be, both are connected to the religion's language of public worship. That is, a personal vision or a private spirituality will derive from or seek to correct the accepted language of the community. Theological reflection will elucidate or attempt to amend the speech of the assembled believers. Even critical analysis of religion by the sympathetic or antagonistic outsider will attend first to the stated speech of the praying community.

DOXOLOGICAL

This book attends to the stated speech of the praying Christian community. Liturgists like to quote the classic dictum *lex orandi, lex credendi*: "as the church prays, so it believes." Although consideration of private imagery and the reconstruction of theological language are essential aspects of the enormous task of ongoing Christian linguistic reform, one must also continually attend to what the churches in public assembly pray and thus purport to believe. In this book, the terms *the liturgy* and *the words of public worship* refer to the regularly recurring and formally approved spoken and sung texts of Christian public worship in the mainline denominations. These texts include what is published in the churches' official books and what is memorized through oral tradition. Of concern as well is the great quantity of material marketed by liturgical entrepreneurs and added to Sunday worship through local judgment, inasmuch as this material, sometimes for better, sometimes for worse, becomes part of the liturgical expression of the faithful.

Liturgical texts include the presider's and the assembly's prayers to God and dialogue with one another, the sung texts of the ordinary and the proper hymns of the day, as well as the specific selection and translation of the psalter and the lectionary. Different denominations exercise more or less control over which words can be included in the liturgy, and in all the churches liturgical texts range from those that are doctrinally approved, for example, the words of institution or the text of baptism, to those eluding any scrutiny whatsoever, perhaps hymn stanzas or the intercessory prayers. All these texts require continual examination. Not only might the words, whether a millennium old or coined yesterday, be inappropriate, unhelpful, or even heretical, but classic formulations, ingrained deeper than critical thought, may prove to be no longer acceptable. Although textual innovations may have more or less prominence in the worship life of particular assemblies, this book focuses on the standard texts of the churches because this language is presented as formative of the faith and is available for scrutiny: as the church prays, so it believes.

Liturgical language includes labels and metaphors for the assembly, sacred space, sacred calendar—indeed, all the things that accompany communal worship. This book, however, attends specifically to doxological language, that is, liturgical speech to and about God. Secular contemporary American English has assisted the church in reforming what has been called horizontal language, that is, speech about humankind, animals, and things. The churches' rapid acceptance of the new translations, such as the New Revised Standard Version of the Bible, illustrates the current consensus concerning this sphere of language. But about speech for God there is little consensus. With what words shall the worshiper address and describe God? Here the secular vernacular can offer little assistance. Yet speech about God is finally the most central concern of the faithful, for who the church's God is, how that God is described, and what believers become in relation to that God are the origin, the substance, and the goal of the faith.

CHRISTIAN

The liturgical God-language addressed in this book is Christian. By *Christian* is meant here the community that affirms the resurrection of

Jesus Christ and enacts the life of God's Spirit by worshiping in assembly and by forming itself to express and convey God's mercy. The Christian community has been shaped by its past of Scripture and tradition. A distinctive part of the core of Christian tradition has been the proclamation of baptismal equality, the countercultural idea that in the resurrected Christ all believers are equals before God and (more debatably) before one another. But the Western world in which that tradition flourished has been androcentric, believing that men were the prototypical humans and that women were inferior and derivative beings. The Christian Scriptures reflect the early struggle to maintain baptismal equality between the sexes while residing in an androcentric culture and using androcentric language. Unfortunately, Christians have usually settled into an accommodation with the culture's androcentric bias. This book joins with many others in the contemporary church to separate cultural androcentrism from the intent of the Spirit for the community of the resurrection.

In every age the Christian community reinterprets its tradition. Although formed by its past, the church sees itself always moving into God's future, able to shed old clothes for new garments more befitting the Spirit's dance. The continual reformation of the church requires careful examination of the words in its past: What did the language of the church mean to convey? Did its speech in fact convey this meaning? What does it presently convey? Continuing to use an old formulation may convey values quite different from, even diametrically opposed to, what was originally intended. The robe of a Franciscan functions differently now than it did in thirteenth-century Assisi. In some things, by restating traditional speech the church remains Christian; what is not so clear is whether or in what areas it loses Christian clarity either by considerably altering traditional speech or by adamantly repeating it.

FEMINIST

Unfortunately, in some circles, even in the church, the word *feminist* is used pejoratively. By *feminist* is meant here the wide range of theory and practice that affirms the full humanity of women. The feminist movement contains considerable diversity in both theory and practice; yet all feminists, female and male, would agree that women are not a derivative species but enjoy full humanity. Feminism has so many varied possibilities clustered in different arrangements that a single continuum is inappropriate to chart its theories and goals. Feminism is better depicted on a grid, on which a certain position may orient different people toward different directions.

A helpful way to conceptualize one axis of this grid uses the terms *maximizers* and *minimizers*. Maximizers, representing an ancient tradition articulated in Aristotle and developed in the so-called separate spheres of the nineteenth century, stress the maximum difference between the sexes. Feminist maximizers value what they see as particularly feminine. Minimizers, in contrast, without denying differences between women and men, proceed instead from an ideal of sexual equality. Both maximizers and minimizers can be anywhere from conservative to radical in their social and religious agendas. The distinction lies not in how revolutionary they are, but in whether they emphasize or deemphasize sexual difference. While no one can deny that a culture displays and usually encourages gender distinctions which may be either biologically essential to the species or socially constructed, this book is more interested in what men and women share in common. Thus this book sides with the minimizers. Not only can sexual stereotypes be potentially as limiting, and perhaps as untrue, as classical androcentrism, but also the Christian community begins in baptismal equality and calls each culture to see beyond its social limitations into the full humanity of the people of God.

A conservative, if not reactionary, position making itself heard proposes that feminist Christianity is an impossibility. Such a position holds that feminist thought and behavior will inevitably divorce itself from Christian trinitarianism and turn to neopagan religion or secular ideology. This conservative Christian voice suspects all feminists as being a negative influence on the faithful community, because first they distort the faith out of their feminist ideas and then leave the church anyway. Indeed, some visible women have argued an increasingly radical feminism and have eventually left the church, judging it essentially and irredeemably sexist. But it may be that the church's reactionary fear of change and misogynist bias helped catapult such feminists out of the church.

Among such conservative Christians are believers who are on some level fundamentalists. Their reverence for the truth of the Bible as God's self-revelation is grounded in devotion to its actual vocabulary.

For these Christians, there is no getting behind the Bible, no relativizing its various messages, and, at least in the areas in which they are passionately concerned, little differentiation between the Spirit of the gospel and the cultural clothing the Bible wears. For some of these Christians, the gospel is not only congruent with androcentrism, but also advocates it. For others, the gospel rightly preached in its biblical terms breaks male-dominated religion and seeks to save the world through divine self-sacrificial love.

While these Christians may rightly be concerned about feminists leaving the church, it is simply myopic to suggest that there can be no such thing as feminist Christians. Thousands of them exist. The literature is replete with serious theological studies by feminist Christians who are examining religious issues from their perspective of faith, and the pews are filled with worshiping women and men who as contemporary Americans are more or less feminists and who are and intend to remain believing and practicing Christians.

All reform movements contain actors who attempt to narrow the stage. Conservatives try to narrow the discussion by excluding the reformers altogether: recall the Council of Trent. The reformers' urgency for the task often leads to splintering the reform into distinctive, sometimes even antagonistic, subgroups: recall the progression of Protestantism. Thus one ought not be surprised that conservative Christians are writing feminists out of the church and that fervent feminist Christians are disagreeing with one another. This book hopes to converse with as wide an array of voices as possible yet toward a specific goal: the consideration of androcentrism in the language to and about God in the approved worship texts of the church.

LANGUAGE

Christianity understood at its inception that the incarnation of God in Christ is best proclaimed in vernacular speech. The search for the vernacular continues, and this ongoing task of translation is complicated by the fact that English in the United States is rapidly changing. A word may no longer convey what it did even a decade ago. Every word, particularly each word about God, must be analyzed to see if it speaks of God and not only of the speaker. Here the task for feminist Christians becomes formidable. It is easy to detect which language speaks more of male power than of divine mercy; it is arduous to offer an alternative that does not merely tout a female counterpart to male power, but moves beyond gender toward the mystery of God.

This book proceeds from the linguistic analysis of Paul Ricoeur, who understands all creative human speech as arising in metaphor. Religious language begins in lively metaphor, babbling a vision, exploding with ecstacy, nurturing human community. Indeed, a believer hopes that such speech originates in God's own creative power. Some of these words, hopefully the ones most accurate to the unique religious faith, become codified in the language of worship and so express the community's identity. Liturgical language is a communal repetition of such metaphoric texts.

The feminist Christian joins with all the teachers of the faith to keep religious language alive; the danger is that the metaphors in doxological language die. When the surprise goes out of the speech, two different outcomes, both problematic, loom as possibilities. First, religious speech can become a taxonomy, memorized theoretical categories that maintain the religious status quo. Participating in the liturgy then becomes an exercise in historic linguistic formulations, a recitation of archaic poetry, rather than a present encounter with the mercy of God. Second, an opposite reaction counters: liturgical planners change the texts of public worship willy-nilly. Here the religious surprise reemerges, but idiosyncratically, perhaps irresponsibly: faithful worshipers may be startled if not shocked by what is laid before them to pray and believe. Thus, Christianity can die from two causes: it can bury itself in archaisms or can dismember itself.

The continuing reform of the church resuscitates the entire range of liturgical language. What should be published as the church's liturgy? Which hymns might be selected? How ought preachers to preach on which readings? How do Christians explain to their children the meaning of the ritual? Evolving reforms breathe the life of the Spirit into the verbal bones littering up the valleys. Christians must describe their religious experience and analyze whether their liturgical speech conveys it. Who is the Christian God, and is the church's doxological language both as evocative and as accurate as possible? All too often in the church, expressive language exists alongside but outside the assembly's speech. The medieval mystics recited the psalms corporately in church and experimented with diverse metaphors privately in their cells. Periodically the two, the approved tradition and its inspired corrective, must meet again, so that the assembly's language can proclaim as well as possible in the vernacular the mercy of God.

It is toward such a goal that this book considers language for God. Organized according to grammatical categories, this book examines the noun *God*; pronouns for the divine; biblical designations, like *Shaddai, Creator*, and *Logos*, divine titles from other religions that were incorporated into the Jewish and Christian traditions; YHWH, the so-called name of God; the myth of the crown; the language of trinitarian doctrine; metaphors that anthropomorphize God; metaphors that objectify God; and verbs. The attempt is to be both devoutly faithful and rigorously critical. Without pretending to be exhaustive, this book hopes by attending especially to doxological language to tackle the most controversial aspect of the liturgical language's feminist reform.

Much of what the church fathers and mothers said on these matters is not only archaic but also counterproductive of contemporary faith. Two statements, however, are helpful: Augustine's realization that human speech and understanding were limited remains a model for even feminist Christians. *Si comprehendis non est Deus*: "If you are comprehending what you are saying, you are not talking about God."[1] Yet he continued writing. Catherine of Siena, overwhelmed by her encounter with the divine, called out, "And what shall I say? I will stutter, 'A-a,' because there is nothing else I know how to say."[2] Yet she continued praying. Accompanied by such Christians as these, we boldly begin our task.

1. Augustine, "Sermons on New Testament Lessons," in *A Select Library of the Nicene and Post-Nicene Fathers*, ed. Philip Schaff (New York: Christian Literature Company, 1888), 6:263.

2. Catherine of Siena, *The Dialogue*, trans. Suzanne Noffke, O.P. (New York: Paulist, 1980), 325.

two

GOD AS A COMMON NOUN

In James Joyce's novel *A Portrait of the Artist as a Young Man*, eight-year-old Stephen Daedalus muses on the divine name:

> God was God's name just as his name was Stephen. *Dieu* was the French for God and that was God's name too; and when anyone prayed to God and said *Dieu* then God knew at once that it was a French person that was praying. But though there were different names for God in all the different languages in the world and God understood what all the people who prayed said in their different languages, still God remained always the same God and God's real name was God.[1]

Stephen, manifesting Joyce's fascination with language, is simply wrong about God's real name being God. Although English capitalizes the word when denoting the god of monotheism, the term *god* is merely a common noun, a label for an entire class of objects, a broad term with a wide field of reference. Because liturgy employs this common noun as if it had specific meaning, we must examine what people actually mean by this word—when they are using it in ways other than its perhaps most common usage as an expletive.

A LOWERCASE *g*

As a common noun, *god* refers to a person or an object of supreme importance in one's life. One's god is the focus of one's life energy, the goal of one's endeavors. When American English uses *god* to denote an

---

1. James Joyce, *A Portrait of the Artist as a Young Man* (New York: Viking, 1964), 16.

individual's passionate attachment to a person or object or endeavor, the usage is somewhat pejorative, as if the nominally monotheistic community views such an object of worship as inappropriate. But with or without the negative connotation, one's god is a private matter, an inclination of the individual, a description of the self, a totally subjective category.

A second usage of *god* denotes one of many male divine beings in a pantheon. We study the gods and goddesses of ancient Aztec religion or contemporary Hinduism. Such a god is one localization of sacred power within a historic religious system. Because polytheism describes both male and female deities, and because our language retains the word *goddess*, the word *god* in this usage keeps its ancient masculine connotation. Many mythologies specifically intend such a masculine identification by ascribing to their gods stereotypical male prowess and hyperactive phallic adventures.

Those who craft public Christian prayer using the address "O God" must realize that the word *god* is a multivalent common noun that denotes both a personal, private attachment to something of questionable worth and an ancient, perhaps archaic, male divinity. Thus *God* used in isolation is less than ideal in liturgical prayer, which is meant to be experienced aurally. The advantage of the word lies in its ability to call up a vast array of religious longings in the assembly. The disadvantage is exactly the same: the countless human desires and deities that arise in the consciousness of those who hear the word *god* make focus on the Christian deity more difficult. Appropriately, contemporary translations and adaptations of the classic Latin collects have clarified the opening *Deus* with a variety of more specifically Christian phrases and biblical verbs, bending the vague address of a deity toward the specific God of faith.

GOD AS THE SURVIVOR OF POLYTHEISM

Capitalizing the word *God* does not necessarily clarify its meaning. Hovering behind monotheistic speech about God is the ghost of monarchical polytheism. It is as if the one God is merely the survivor of an extinct species, the last of a breed. Christians must attend to the problems that result from the fact that polytheism underlies both their cultural thought patterns and their religious tradition, both the Greco-Roman and the Hebrew worlds.

Study of ancient Greek myth suggests that the primordial generation of named powers—Gaia, Chaos, Eros, Uranos—were objectifications of the inexplicable powers of the universe. From these vague entities developed personifications of more specific power and rights. Gaia, the primordial force for bearing all life, was succeeded by Hera, the jealous queen and manipulative wife of the male sovereign. By the time of classical Greek literature, the pantheon of deities both mirrored and legitimated the hierarchical Greek social structure.[2]

In later classical Greek philosophy, the legends of the pantheon were ridiculed or dismissed by sophisticated thinkers. Socrates goaded his neighbors about their anthropomorphic deities: he urged critical thinkers to see beyond the many deities to a single overarching principle of power.[3] Aristotle began his discussion of the Prime Mover not with ancient legends of the gods and goddesses but with a logical exposition of motion in the universe.[4] Thus Greek philosophy simplified the many deities into the One. By the Christian era, Roman literature praised Zeus/Jupiter not only as the father of all gods but also as the father of all worshipers, the source of all human authority—indeed, the one God over all the world.[5] Primordial sacred power had evolved through a pantheon of personalities into a single personal locus of authority. This single deity, however, was still popularly called Jupiter. That is, monotheism has in its backbone polytheism, and centuries of ancient poetic religious language are retained in the later more philosophically sophisticated religious system.

A similar pattern lies behind the Hebrew Scriptures. Studies of Ugaritic myth have demonstrated that the Canaanites venerated various deities, including El, the creator of the universe and the father of the gods, and Baal, the storm god and master of the earthly order.[6] El was believed to rule from the holy mountain over a council of the deities,

---

2. Walter Burkert, *Greek Religion*, trans. John Raffan (Cambridge, Mass.: Harvard University Press, 1985), 246–50.

3. Plato, "Euthyphro," in *The Collected Dialogues*, ed. Edith Hamilton and Huntington Cairns (New York: Pantheon Books, 1961), 174–85.

4. Aristotle, *Metaphysics X–XIV*, trans. Hugh Tredennick, Loeb Classical Library 18 (Cambridge, Mass.: Harvard University Press, 1935), 141–51.

5. Burkert, *Greek Religion*, 129–30.

6. E. Theodore Mullen Jr., *The Assembly of the Gods*, Harvard Semitic Monographs 24 (Chico, Calif.: Scholars Press, 1980), 109–10.

who heeded his judgment and praised his majesty. Psalm 82 is one biblical poem in which the Hebrew high god is honored for excellence in presiding over the council of lesser deities. That the Hebrew word for God *Elohim* is a plural form of the Canaanite *El* demonstrates a development from many diverse gods through an organized pantheon to a single god. Yet the one god still evidences its legendary past. The Hebrew Scriptures proscribe anthropomorphic depiction of their one god. Images are prohibited (which very prohibition suggests that images were in fact sculpted), and YHWH is neither exposing her breasts nor brandishing his phallus. Yet the vestiges of anthropomorphic polytheism remain. In Exodus 19 God resides on top of the sacred mountain; in Exodus 15 YHWH, like El, is a warrior conquering the enemy; in Psalm 19 God, like Baal, is a storm god raining down terror. Eventually the literal belief in this language subsides; for example, Jewish and Christian tradition turns the lesser deities of the old pantheons into angels. But the ancient monarchical polytheism undergirds much Judeo-Christian divine imagery to this day.

Hebrew monotheism may have been a gradual development in reaction to the polytheisms of the ancient Near East, or it may have been a historic breakthrough made by a specific visionary. But evidence shows that the move from goddesses and gods to one God mirrored (and also legitimated) a tightening of gender roles within the community and a persistent assignment of the masculine to divinity. This occurred in Judaism even though its monotheism asserted that God is not sexed.[7] In pluralistic conceptions of divinity, deities of both genders participate in all areas of natural and civilized life. Monotheism as described during the Israelite monarchy elevated only the masculine to divinity, effectively demoting the feminine to earthly or nongodly concerns.[8]

Recent examination of the history of medieval Marian devotion shows that while Christianity developed in the El/Jupiter tradition, at least some Christians revived adoration of the divine feminine. We know that statues of Isis nursing Horus served as models for statues of Mary

7. Tikva Frymer-Kensky, *In the Wake of the Goddesses: Women, Culture, and the Biblical Transformation of Pagan Myth* (New York: Free Press, 1992), 188–89.

8. Judith Ochshorn, *The Female Experience and the Nature of the Divine* (Bloomington: Indiana University Press, 1981), 14–15, passim.

nursing Jesus and that Christian churches honoring Mary were built on sites of goddess worship.[9] Pagan rituals to the grain goddess evolved into legends and rites of female saints including Mary herself.[10] This transfer of the divine feminine from goddesses to the cults of the Virgin and female saints meant that the male supremacy in monotheism was countered, if not in theology, at least in devotion. Some manifestations of Roman Catholicism are best understood as resurgent polytheism, in which the high god and the dominant goddess reign over a panoply of angels and saints who each bears specific power and authority over the worshipers. In the United States, the Roman church's refusal to Christianize the native American female powers and the necessity to coexist with a sometimes belligerent Protestant majority formed an American Catholicism in which female divine power was somewhat diminished.

In Protestantism the feminine divine has been smashed, and thus the androcentrism of its vestigial polytheism can be overpowering. With all the female divinity of the primary goddess and the lesser female powers obliterated, all that remained in the Protestant religious imagination was El/Jupiter, the sky-dwelling lawgiver and the father of all. The rise in Protestantism of the image and roles of women cannot be credited to any teaching about divine gender, but rather to various cultural patterns in the Reformation churches: for example, their emphasis on literacy, their valuing of individual freedom, the people's rising economic status, and a residual anticlericalism. Contemporary reforms about gender language for God do well to heed this historic development and so avoid the misapprehension that only goddess worship ensures power for women.

God imagined as Jupiter the Survivor constitutes an enormous problem in Christian prayer. Many people educated in the United States have studied polytheistic or animistic religions more than they ever studied Christian theology, and the current interest in multiculturally diverse curriculums will enlarge the polytheistic imagination of worshiping Christians. By postulating many deities, polytheism requires

---

9. Marina Warner, *Alone of All Her Sex: The Myth and the Cult of the Virgin Mary* (New York: Knopf, 1976), 193–95.

10. Pamela Berger, *The Goddess Obscured: Transformation of the Grain Protectress From Goddess to Saint* (Boston: Beacon, 1985), 49–143.

that the lone individual or the group itself effect human health and salvation. In polytheism, one must know which deity is the most powerful in each situation; one must know how to balance the conflicting divine authorities; and, as polytheisms usually include deities who dispense misery and death, one must survive in spite of superhuman powers of evil. Polytheism contradicts the two major tenets of Christianity, namely, that one benevolent God is supreme in the universe and that evil has been conquered in Christ. While divine grace is difficult for humans to accept under any conditions, a polytheistic imagination poses explicit obstacles to Christian faith.

The psalter is a prime example of residual polytheism in Christian liturgy. The psalms were revived simultaneously to the churches' attempt to neutralize the male power of the ancient divine monarch. Ironically, these ancient poems more than any other liturgical genre are marked by an overabundance of male polytheistic language. That God the king presides over a council of lesser deities, rains down angry thunderbolts, leads the tribal armies to victory, judges from a throne—these are all leftovers from monarchical polytheism. Although the so-called enthronement psalms are usually appointed for festivals honoring Christ, the place of Psalm 95 as a primary morning psalm requires contemporary Christians to acclaim daily that the God YHWH is El, the head of the Canaanite pantheon. (For those worshipers who do not know about El, the imagery in Psalm 95 will teach them.)

The contemporary revival of the psalter can be credited to several phenomena: the central role that Roman Catholic monasticism, with its tradition of the daily office, has played in Christian liturgical reform; the rediscovery of the Calvinist charism for psalm-singing; and current biblical interest in metaphor. In spite of the good accruing to the liturgy from this revival, the church cannot blindly memorize the psalter without carefully investigating the image of God therein. While some psalms are replete with diverse and multivalent images for God, others are so marked by unreflective ancient polytheism that they might be judged counterproductive for Christian use.[11] The praise of a warrior

11. Translations of the psalter such as *Psalter for the Christian People*, ed. Gordon Lathrop and Gail Ramshaw (Collegeville, Minn.: Liturgical Press, 1993), while eliminating male references to the divine, do not expurgate the residual polytheism in the Psalms.

deity who gleefully slaughters one's enemies, the notion that the desires of one's tribe constitute divine justice, the uncritical use of male imagery for God—these are several themes in the psalter that must give Christians pause.

GOD AS A SUPERHUMAN BEING

The change from Gaia, the feminine divine power of life, to Hera, the nagging queen of Olympus, demonstrates that the characters in the Greek pantheon combined personified divine power with glorified human tendencies. Zeus represents both the inexplicable might of the thunder and the shenanigans of a petty tyrant. Today's scientific mentality, however, urges us to identify natural causes for thunder. Thus what is left of God is a larger-than-life human creature. God becomes not the survivor of polytheism, one power beyond all other powers, but a benign older relative who thinks pleasant thoughts without effecting much good. Perhaps this alteration in religious thought logically evolved in an age of humanism. If the human being is understood as the center of consciousness and meaning, then imagining a deity as anything other than a somewhat more magnificent example of human life may be difficult.

An example of this humanization of God can be seen in the development of language in Christian hymnody. In Reformation hymnody, Jesus can help humans, not because he is human, but because he is divine. In Johann Rist's hymn of 1641, on Good Friday "Gott selbst ist tot," God's very self is dead. In Johann Franck's "Jesu, meine Freude," published in 1655, Jesus is divine might, humanity's connection to the power of God over the forces of Satan and death. The line in modern translations, "truest friend to me," is inaccurate to the original German text.[12] Jesus as a friend is a later idea: "What a friend we have in Jesus," wrote Joseph Scriven in 1865. Scriven makes clear that Jesus, as the Christian's friend, will at least offer comfort in distress. The nineteenth-century scholarly interest in the historical Jesus gave theological support to an increasingly human savior. In the twentieth century the idea that Jesus has been in humanity's shoes has evolved into the idea that God

---

12. The original German and English translations of these hymns are printed in parallel columns in W. G. Polack, *The Handbook to the Lutheran Hymnal*, 3d rev. ed. (St. Louis: Concordia, 1942), 131, 248.

walks by one's side. This century has turned from Jesus, a friend of sinners, toward God the Friend, who is praised for being a companion and is asked for advice.[13] The movement over the Christian centuries has been from a mighty God to a mighty Christ to a friendly Jesus to a friendly God. Much recent intercessory prayer assumes and addresses only a superhuman God. In place of pleas for heavenly intervention or divine mercy, one hears phrases asking God to "help us realize that." According to such a petition, human beings will solve the world's problems, particularly if inspired by God, who represents the highest human thoughts. Such prayer often suggests that these high human thoughts are fortunately shared by the person crafting the intercessory prayer. These prayers can finally deteriorate into exercises in consciousness-raising, with neither a mighty God nor a friendly Jesus believed to have divine powers over the state of the world.

Anthropomorphic talk of divinity—"the LORD God walking in the garden at the time of the evening breeze," for example—could lead, one suspects, to a humanized God. A religion of incarnation is especially prone to imagining a superhuman deity. Christians came to draw first symbolic images and later naturalistic portraits of Jesus, and this licensed Christian artists to draw portraits of God.[14] That countless Christians sat for hours before depictions of God as two men and a bird, despite any profound theological intention of such art, must be in a great part responsible for the demotion of the divine from primordial power itself to merely an oversized male. Little difference exists between people in a monarchy depicting God as a bearded king and people in an agricultural tribe honoring a statue of a bull. (Mercifully the Sistine Chapel with Michelangelo's fresco of creation depicting God's and Adam's fingers nearly touching is not a place of public eucharistic worship.) In some contemporary spiritualities the superhuman is female or androgynous, but that does not solve the problem; it only gives a broader base to a humanized God.

13. Sallie McFague, *Models of God: Theology for an Ecological, Nuclear Age* (Philadelphia: Fortress, 1987), 157–80.

14. The thirteenth-century *Bible Moralisée* is an early example of drawing Christ and God as identical-looking males, one dressed in red robes, the other in blue. A facsimile edition, Codex Vindobonensis 2554, Reihe Codices Selecti XL, is available in several libraries in the United States.

The language of God-as-person has contributed to this divine demotion. The orthodox theological category of *person* has failed to convey its original meaning. In place of its intended philosophical meaning has arisen consideration of a personal God. Christianity has maintained that, distinct from the uncaring deities of some polytheisms or the aloof deist's God, God loves each human person. This belief has licensed Christians to talk as if, like a human person, God has one personality, or three individual personalities, and is capable of interpersonal relationship. The "three-personed God" becomes "God is a person."[15] God ends up a superperson whose powers and preferences can be deduced from one's knowledge of regular human persons.

THE *IMAGO DEI*

The history of the interpretation of the *imago dei* offers a striking illustration of the humanization of God. Christian theologians from Paul onward have offered differing explications of the enigmatic phrase in Genesis 1:27 that human beings were created in the divine image.[16] Early Christian theologians speculated, as did the rabbis, whether a difference exists between *image* and *likeness*. Some said the image was as if on a coin, others as if in a mirror. Some believed the image was lost completely in the Fall, others that it was only obscured. Still others began their consideration with Christology, asserting that only Christ is the perfect image of God.

The consensus through much of the Christian tradition up through Thomas Aquinas was that because the divine nature is rational, the *imago dei* is rationality. Gregory of Nyssa followed Philo in speculating that only the primordial human creature had divine rationality, which was lost as the creature was differentiated into two sexes.[17] While

15. Piet Schoonenberg, "God as Person(al)," in *A Personal God?*, ed. Edward Schillebeeckx and Bas van Iersel, *Concilium* 103 (New York: Seabury, 1977), 81–82.

16. See Kari Elisabeth Børresen, ed., *Image of God and Gender Models in Judeo-Christian Tradition* (Oslo: Solum, 1991), and Anthony A. Hoekema, *Created in God's Image* (Grand Rapids: Eerdmans, 1986).

17. Gregory of Nyssa, "On the Making of Man," in *A Select Library of Nicene and Post-Nicene Fathers*, ed. Philip Schaff and Henry Wace, 2d series (New York: Christian Literature Company, 1894), 5:405–6.

Augustine proposed a trinity in the human being of memory, understanding, and will as the image of the divine,[18] he is more remembered
for his musings that because of his reason, the male is in the image of
God, and that the female can be in the image of God only in relation
to a male.[19]

Other meanings than rationality were proposed in the Reformation.
Martin Luther considered the lost image to be humankind's willing
orientation toward God.[20] John Calvin believed it to be humanity's
primordial moral perfection.[21] Various proposals continue until the
present.[22] Historical critics, for example, have suggested that the writer
of Genesis used the phrase to signify upright posture or royal representation. A current theory, considering Mesopotamian and Egyptian
religious iconography, suggests that a specific creature in which the
deity was manifest was depicted as the image of that god.[23]

Throughout the controversy, how theologians defined the *imago dei*
followed from either their conception of God or their hope for humanity.
That is, the theologians identify as the *imago dei* whatever part of the
biblical record or human anthropology or theological assertion that is
most central to their argument. If human rationality is the key to one's
argument, then the image of God is rationality. If critics wish to
elaborate on the royal metaphor, then divine representation is the *imago
dei*. In recent ecofeminist thought, the image of God in humankind
is the responsibility for ecological care and healing.[24]

Recently the *imago dei* is coming to be accepted as a statement about
gender. Perhaps this roots back to 1 Corinthians 11:7, where Paul,

18. Augustine, "On the Holy Trinity," in *A Select Library of Nicene and Post-Nicene Fathers*, ed. Philip Schaff (Buffalo: Christian Literature Company, 1887), 3:143.

19. Augustine, "On the Holy Trinity," 159.

20. Martin Luther, *Lectures on Genesis*, in *Luther's Works*, ed. Jaroslav Pelikan (St. Louis: Concordia, 1958), 1:63.

21. John Calvin, *Institutes of the Christian Religion*, ed. John T. McNeill, trans. Ford Lewis Battles, Library of Christian Classics 20 (Philadelphia: Westminster, 1960), 1:188.

22. Gunnlauger A. Jonsson, *The Image of God: Genesis 1:26-28 in a Century of Old Testament Research* (Stockholm: Almqvist and Wiksell, 1988).

23. Edward M. Curtis, "Image of God (OT)," *The Anchor Bible Dictionary*, ed. David Noel Freedman (New York: Doubleday, 1992), 3:390.

24. Rosemary Radford Ruether, *Gaia and God: An Ecofeminist Theology of Earth Healing* (San Francisco: HarperCollins, 1992), 222.

struggling to distinguish men's and women's rights in the assembly, postulates that males, rather than all human beings, are the image of God. For the most part, the Western tradition suggested this more obliquely than Paul did: God is rationality; according to Aristotelian anthropology, males are more rational than females; consequently more of the divine image exists in males than in females.[25]

No consensus on the gender of the *imago dei* has been achieved. From Paul to the present, theologians have vacillated between the notion that androcentrism reflects the divine nature and the belief that baptism brings sexual parity. For example, Aquinas, although reserving ordination for males, specifically argues that both men and women are created in the image of God.[26] But for Karl Barth, the Aristotelian notion of male supremacy is fundamental to understanding human life within the orders of creation. The I-Thou relationship between God and humankind is imagined in terms of the relationship males and females know together.[27] Thus the duality of male and female and the inherent superiority of the male are essential to God's being and nature and to the *imago dei*. Phyllis Trible countered Barth's androcentric suggestion with her influential exegesis of Genesis 1. For Trible, the *imago dei* is the divine nature of gender equality: "Procreation is shared by humankind with the animal world; sexuality is not. . . . To describe male and female, then, is to perceive the image of God."[28] To keep the image of God from masculinity, God becomes supernaturally both male and female.

The present time is marked by interest not in rationality, but in sexuality. Popular religious literature indicates how prevalent the identification of the image of God with the gender of God has become.[29]

25. See Elizabeth A. Morelli, "The Question of Woman's Experience of God," in *Speaking the Christian God: The Holy Trinity and the Challenge of Feminism*, ed. Alvin F. Kimel Jr. (Grand Rapids: Eerdmans, 1992), 222–36, for one woman's rejection of the equation between rationality and masculinity.

26. Thomas Aquinas, *Summa Theologiae*, 1a.93.4.

27. Karl Barth, *Church Dogmatics* (Edinburgh: T. & T. Clark, 1960), III, 1:184–87.

28. Phyllis Trible, *God and the Rhetoric of Sexuality* (Philadelphia: Fortress, 1978), 15, 21.

29. A few examples: Jann Aldredge Clanton, *In Whose Image? God and Gender* (New York: Crossroad, 1990); Eleanor Rae and Bernice Marie-Daly, *Created in Her Image: Models of the Feminine Divine* (New York: Crossroad, 1990); and *Made in God's Image*, a statement about sexism published by the Roman Catholic bishops of New Zealand.

Unfortunately the church is falling prey to an interpretation of the *imago dei* based in sexuality. To argue that the *imago dei* means androgyny is an inadequate response to historic androcentrism, because androgyny reinforces the problematic interpretation that the *imago dei* has anything to do with gender at all.[30]

The suggestion that God's image is about sexuality is finally not convincing. One quality human beings share with countless other species of animals and plants is sexual differentiation. Yet the writer of Genesis claims that the image of God is held uniquely by human beings, and this claim is what gives the church its interest in the *imago dei*. That the writer of Genesis could believe or the Christian tradition deduce that the divine quality enjoyed solely by humankind is gender differentiation is illogical and unsupportable.

The conundrum over the *imago dei* illustrates the church's tendency to humanize God. Whether the image of God is touted as rationality or morality or either masculine or androgynous sexuality, it is a human quality that, glorified as the *imago dei*, the theologian projects into the sky. The *imago dei* is then returned to earth, because God, conceived according to that specific human quality, is said to have created humankind to contain this quality. The circularity of the argument would be humorous were it not so pernicious. The Jewish tradition—in keeping with its tendencies to avoid speculation about God and to affirm divine transcendence—has made very little of this enigmatic phrase from Genesis.

THE TASK FOR CHRISTIAN PRAYER

For Christians to use the common noun *God* with clarity, the word must be overhauled. Christians must re-deify their conception of God, and Christian language must reflect a renewed appreciation of divinity. Such deification requires degendering the word *God*. This task is not new to Christianity. During the fourth century the creative theologians often called the Cappadocian Fathers had to answer to the accusation that the Trinity they were describing was none other than masculine tritheism. Gregory of Nazianzus is premier among many Christian

---

30. Phyllis A. Bird, "Sexual Differentiation and Divine Image in the Genesis Creation Texts," in *Image of God and Gender Models in Judeo-Christian Tradition*, 11–31.

theologians who dismiss any meaning behind traditional masculine
language for God. He wrote, "Maybe you would consider our God to
be a male, according to the same argument, because he is called God
the Father, and that Deity is feminine, for the gender of the word, and
Spirit neuter, because It has nothing to do with generation!"[31] But
sarcasm aside, language creates reality. In spite of the theological tradition that continued to claim a God beyond gender, many writers
attest that for most modern people, the word *God* remains a masculine
term.

Rosemary Radford Ruether has advocated the neologism *God/ess*
with the hope that its androgynous overtones will drown out the
masculine blare of *God*.[32] *God/ess*, however, emphasizes gender, encouraging the believer to image a deity of both genders rather than a
deity beyond gender. Aurally, the word is indistinguishable from *goddess*.
Other attempts to give feminine connotation to God include alternate
use of *Goddess* and the neologism *Womangod*.[33] In a century obsessed
with sexuality, it is difficult to image a being beyond sexuality; we
more easily fantasize a supersexual being, one more fully sexual than
ourselves. Little is available to offer confidence that further incorporating sexuality into divinity will ultimately enrich our image of God.
Sexuality is a method of reproduction among species that will otherwise
die. When in paganism divinity is part of the created order, sexuality
is constitutive also of divine life, but in monotheism, it is not only
illogical but theologically inappropriate to ascribe sexuality to divinity.

The word *God* is not the only term degendered in the twentieth
century. American English is removing the gender designation of many
occupational titles, which is what the word *God* is. *Principal, doctor*,
or *priest*, for example, are no longer masculine terms. *Firefighter, mail
carrier*, and *flight attendant* are titles that speak inclusively of occupations
no longer filled solely by males or females. The feminine ending *-ess*,
as in the archaic word *poetess*, is largely abandoned, because it signaled
not only female sex but diminutive status. Publishers of children's

31. Gregory of Nazianzus, "The Fifth Theological Oration: On the Spirit," in
A Select Library of Nicene and Post-Nicene Fathers, 2d series, 7:320.

32. Rosemary Radford Ruether, *Sexism and God-Talk: Toward a Feminist Theology*
(Boston: Beacon, 1983), 45–46.

33. Mary Kathleen Speegle Schmitt, *Seasons of the Feminine Divine: Christian
Feminist Prayers for the Liturgical Cycle* (Boston: Beacon, 1993), 64, passim.

textbooks, for example, maintain rigid linguistic style sheets, enforcing a degendering of titles, occupations, and personality inclinations. Such degendering will take many decades to accomplish. One still hears talk of whether the president of the United States could be a woman, indicating that in many minds the title *president* is a male term. But current progress proves that American English can change in fundamental ways. The desire that the word *doctor* be degendered has met the social reality that many doctors are women. Christians need more than a benign desire that the word *God*, as well as the reality worshiped, be degendered. A degendered God will be effected only if Christians actually believe in one.

The task of degendering the word *God* is massive. Pronouns, designations, doctrinal speech, metaphors, and personifications of the deity must speak more truthfully of a God who according to Christian tradition is beyond gender. We need to whitewash murals that depict God as a male creature. Children's books must be devoid of demeaning portraiture of God. Light streaming from behind a cloud is no profound picture of God, but it is surely more Christian than a drawing of Jupiter.

The second task is unhumanizing the connotations of the term *God*. Language, such as "God the friend," is helpful as a partial corrective to other inadequate categories, such as "God the judge." That God is wholly other, not like human beings, and beyond our comprehension in every way—this truth is lost when the divine is replaced by the superhuman. Although different religions offer quite divergent ways to conceive reality, the Christian worldview postulates a distinction between the divine and the human. When anthropomorphisms succeed in containing God, we have no God; we have instead a glorified image of ourselves. It may be illuminating for Christians to adapt Jewish practice of indicating divine ineffability by writing the word as *G-d*.[34] But such practice, while formative for the reader, is ineffectual in aural liturgical usage.

Christian prayer is an enactment of the belief in a God beyond humanity, a deity who promises to visit the world with peace and justice. Prayer assumes that God's creative power is still operative and

---

34. Elisabeth Schüssler Fiorenza, *But She Said: Feminist Practices of Biblical Interpretation* (Boston: Beacon, 1992), adopts this practice.

that the world needs to be grounded in God's mercy. Intercessions can affirm both human responsibility and divine love, but intercessions ought never be demoted into bulletin boards or lists of self-identified causes. Intercessions are a theological enterprise, an exploration into the mind of God, a weekly articulation of faith in divine mercy and might. Petitions read out in the presence of a superhuman being are not Christian prayer.

Augustine wrote about the word *God* in a manner that now sounds charmingly naive:

> God, although nothing worthy of His greatness can be said of Him, . . . has desired us through the medium of our own words to rejoice in His praise. For on this principle it is that He is called *Deus*. For the sound of those two syllables in itself conveys no true knowledge of His nature; but yet all who know the Latin tongue are led, when that sound reaches their ears, to think of a nature supreme in excellence and eternal in existence.[35]

Whether Augustine was correct that the very sound of the Latin word *Deus* evoked awe in its hearers, the American English word *God* surely does not. To polytheists and neopagans, the word means one of countless manifestations of male divine power; to humanists, the word evokes the highest aspirations of civilization; to some people, the word suggests a retired monarch; to others, a human presence. Yet Christianity proclaims a God who is "supreme in excellence and eternal in existence," and it is such a God that the Christian's words must attempt to express. While the task is considerable, there is no reason to fear that in current vernacular such proclamation is impossible.

---

35. Augustine, "On Christian Doctrine," in *A Select Library of Nicene and Post-Nicene Fathers*, 2:523.

three

PRONOUNS AND THE CHRISTIAN GOD

In the English language, the plural pronoun *they* is gender-neutral, but singular pronouns are sex-specific: *he, she, it.* Linguistic historian Dennis Baron has written of this happenstance, "It is doubtful that any one semantic gap in any language has ever received the attention that reformers over the years have lavished on our lack of a common-gender pronoun in English."[1] The Christian church, along with many areas of the culture, is now grappling with the sex-specific singular pronoun. The task in this chapter is to consider how the singular pronoun has functioned in reference to the God of biblical religion, what is happening to the pronoun *he* in contemporary American English, and how Christians are newly to think about pronomial reference to God.

THE DIVINE PRONOUN IN BIBLICAL RELIGION

Many languages have what is called grammatical gender; that is, all nouns and pronouns are assigned to one of three gender categories: feminine, masculine, and neuter. These assignments may seem natural, as in the noun *mother* being in the feminine gender; logical, as in *milk* being feminine in Spanish; arbitrary, as in *chair* being feminine in French; or illogical, as in *young girl* being neuter in German. Some scholars attempt to ascertain why a certain inanimate object was assigned its specific gender, but there is no consensus in contemporary linguistic theory concerning the origins of gender in language. Such theories tend to reveal more about the sexual stereotypes of their framers than of any

1. Dennis Baron, *Grammar and Gender* (New Haven: Yale University Press, 1986), 8.

historical accuracy about language formation.[2] In those living Western languages with grammatical gender, however, no meaningfulness accompanies the gender designation. That *chair* is feminine does not mean that the chair has female sexuality or that it is related to a characteristically feminine realm in the social order. *Chair* is feminine grammatically only.

In addition to grammatical gender, which is an arbitrary system organizing the language, there is natural gender, when an animate being with specific sexuality is so termed. To complicate matters, however, especially in the discourse of religion, metaphorical gender also exists. In poetic uses of language, which abound in religion, gender often functions metaphorically. "Joy to the world, the Lord is come,/ Let earth receive her King," wrote Isaac Watts, as if the earth were feminine. The pattern in Western metaphor is culturally stereotypical, reflecting the Greco-Roman belief that the masculine is dominant and rational and the feminine recessive and emotional. Prose in the United States today contains vestiges of metaphorical gender: some sailors may still call a ship "she," some politicians their nation "she," some Christians the church "she."

All the languages formative in the Judeo-Christian tradition—Hebrew, Aramaic, Greek, Latin, and the European languages of the Middle Ages—had grammatical gender for nouns and pronouns. We cannot know to what degree thoughtful speakers of those languages placed any reality in these gender distinctions. We know that the noun *god* maintained masculine gender for Christian speakers and writers, even when those very Christians explicitly taught against any meaningfulness of such gender designations. Recall Gregory of Nazianzus ridiculing those who would draw from the gender designation in language a notion of actual sexuality within God.[3] Aquinas defended the expression *Qui est (the One Who Is)* as the most appropriate name for God; disregarding any significance in his use of the masculine relative pronoun, he judged that the term "does not signify any particular form, but rather existence itself."[4] Like Jewish theologians, Christian theologians

2. Ibid., 91.

3. Gregory of Nazianzus, "The Fifth Theological Oration: On the Spirit," in *A Select Library of Nicene and Post-Nicene Fathers,* ed. Philip Schaff and Henry Wace, 2d series (New York: Christian Literature Company, 1894), 5:520.

4. Thomas Aquinas, *Summa Theologiae,* 1a.13.11.

have consistently denied gender designations to God; yet they continued until recent decades apparently without concern to employ masculine pronouns for God. It is likely that their use of *he* indicates to what great degree God was unconsciously imaged as a superman.

It is painfully evident that, the arguments of Gregory and Aquinas notwithstanding, the use of the masculine pronoun has come to signify for countless believers either actual male sexuality in God or a divine androcentrism. For some speakers and writers of the biblical religions, use of the masculine pronoun was seen as a theologically appropriate corrective to the language and imagery of neighboring goddess worship. Still other Christians have claimed that the masculine pronoun was, is, or with goodwill can be considered generic, thus serving theological speech well. Probably many Christian speakers have not yet given the matter much thought. Meanwhile, other Christians have erased from their language the divine masculine pronoun and are more or less militant in urging this reform. Recently published liturgical materials have radically reduced or wholly eliminated use of any divine masculine pronouns in newly composed or translated texts.[5]

THE PRONOUN IN CONTEMPORARY AMERICAN ENGLISH

Anglo-Saxon, the linguistic family spoken in England in the year 1000, was an inflected language with grammatical gender like its Germanic antecedents. Contemporary readers must approach Anglo-Saxon as a foreign language, finding it closer to modern German or Dutch than to modern English. After the Norman invasion, Anglo-Saxon became the language of the conquered and the uneducated, and its consequent simplification led to abandonment of most of its inflected endings. Through the centuries English has become a less and less inflected language. The subjective mood, for example, is nearly obsolete. We can still see the old system of declining and conjugating in such words as *mouse-mice, go-went-gone*, and *he-she-it*. But modern American English functions almost totally with the simplest gender system, what grammarians call natural gender. That is, an animate female is *she*, an animate male is *he*, and all singular else is *it*.

5. See, for example, *Book of Common Worship* (Louisville: Westminster/John Knox Press, 1993).

The requirement of knowing the sex of any animated being in order to frame sentences properly has long been recognized as a deficiency in the English language. Linguistic historians have chronicled several centuries of the search for a sex-neutral personal pronoun. Baron lists eighty proposals offered since the early eighteenth century for such a singular pronoun.[6] In 1976 the National Council of Teachers of English prepared guidelines for managing available options in more sex-fair ways.[7] Current handbooks of the language contradict old-style advice that sexual specificity was important to speech and instead advise methods of sex-fair and sex-neutral speech.[8] Prominent publishers, especially of children's textbooks, have for twenty years maintained strict style sheets that not only challenge the sexually stereotypical attitudes underlying the language and its metaphors, but regulate pronoun usage.[9]

The argument that *he* is generic is becoming extinct. An early articulation of this usage was the 1850 British Act of Parliament legitimizing *he* as generic in governmental proceedings, but considerable doubt exists whether the masculine was ever genuinely generic. "All men are created equal" did not mean in any practical matter to include women in the rights men enjoyed. It appears that benign statements, such as "God forgives man his sins," may have used masculine words generically; yet the generic interpretation could quickly yield to androcentrism, as in "He can seek ordination." Studies indicate that in current usage the masculine pronoun is understood as referring to males unless the hearer can provide the wider bisexual context.[10]

6. Baron, *Grammar and Gender,* 205–9.

7. A. Pace Nilsen, et al., *Sexism and Language* (Urbana, Ill.: National Council of Teachers of English, 1977), 182–91.

8. See, for example, Casey Miller and Kate Swift, *The Handbook of Nonsexist Writing,* 2d ed. (New York: Harper & Row, 1980).

9. See, for example, "Guidelines for Equal Treatment of the Sexes in the McGraw-Hill Book Company Publications," McGraw-Hill, 1974; "Guidelines for Creating Positive Sexual and Racial Images in Educational Materials," Macmillan, 1975; "Eliminating Stereotypes," Houghton Mifflin, 1982; "Guidelines for Improving the Images of Women in Textbooks," Scott, Foresman & Company, 1974.

10. Edward H. Bendix, "Linguistic Models as Political Symbols: Gender and the Generic 'He' in English," in *Language, Sex and Gender,* Annals of the New York Academy of Sciences 327 (New York: New York Academy of Sciences, 1979), 23–39.

But whether one believes that the generic masculine ever existed, one must conclude it is now nearly dead, and current attempts to employ it often create unclarity. Although the move to sex-neutral terminology is firmly in place in the United States, the singular pronoun remains a conundrum. With nouns, language has moved from sex-specific terms, such as *stewardess*, to sex-neutral terms, such as *flight attendant*. In some areas, reconstructive degenderization has been possible; that is, words are coined to fit specific needs. An example is *chair*, or *chairperson*, for *chairman*. But in the search for an inclusive pronoun, contextual degenderization is under way.[11] That is, rather than invent a new singular pronoun, context is increasingly allowing the use of the plural pronoun, *they-their-them*, as a singular. Handbooks advocate either returning to the use of *they* as a singular or recasting the sentence to eliminate the pronoun.[12] Social necessity is changing pronoun use, although none of the eighty clever (and not so clever) proposals for a sex-neutral pronoun has succeeded.

OPTIONS FOR RELIGIOUS LANGUAGE

The abandonment of grammatical gender in contemporary North American English forces Christian language to alter its traditional terminology. If increasingly *he* not only connotes but actually denotes male sexuality, it becomes a matter of idolatry to continue to refer to the divine as *he*. Were a neologism coined and accepted, Christians could move to this new usage, as they moved from *Negro* to *black* to *African American* with relative goodwill and reasonable speed. Yet without such a neologism, the options are problematic.

While the Christian tradition has sometimes referred to the Spirit of God as *it*, a move to use *it* as the normal divine pronoun in liturgical speech is unlikely. Pseudo-Dionysius used *it* in reference to the Godhead with admirable awe,[13] and Sallie McFague, concerned whether any anthropocentrism in language about God is tenable in a postmodern

11. Elizabeth Lane Beardsley, "Degenderization," in *Sexist Language: A Modern Philosophical Analysis*, ed. Mary Vetterling-Braggin (Totowa, N.J.: Rowman & Littlefield, 1981), 155–60.

12. See, for example, Miller and Swift, *Handbook of Nonsexist Writing*, 43–58.

13. Pseudo-Dionysius, "The Divine Names," in *Pseudo-Dionysius: The Complete Words*, trans. Colm Luibheid (New York: Paulist, 1987), 54–56; "The Mystical Theology," 141.

scientific worldview, suggests *it* as the best option for Christian reflection. [14] Christian liturgy as we know it, however, presumes that
God is a being who continually relates to human persons. Thus while
perhaps useful for theological reflection, the objectification implied by
it will inhibit its adoption in praise of God.

Contemporary grammarians, realizing that *they* is used regularly in
spoken and informal written language as a singular generic pronoun,
predict or even advocate that *they* receive sanction as a singular. Even
when such a linguistic change occurs, however, *they* would be an unacceptable pronoun for God. Christianity must always struggle against
a popular tritheism that imagines a committee of three in the skies.
In the effort to believe and teach the fundamental tenet of monotheism,
they would be counterproductive.

She is increasingly being used to refer to God. Some of this usage
expresses a popular backlash against the centuries of *he*, in much the
same way that the biblical usage saw *he* as a corrective to the *she* of
goddess worship. Other Christians are being influenced by the current
popularity of goddess worship, some of which is a serious revival of
ancient polytheism. Bookstores are stocked with materials proposing
that the ancient honoring of the earth goddess or the mothering principle will ensure wholeness to contemporary women and ecological
responsibility toward the planet. [15] Some *she* usage, then, is entering
Christian speech by osmosis and through inattention to doctrinal clarity.

Serious Christian theologians, however, are also proposing use of
she. Most notably, Elizabeth Johnson has argued that the feminine
pronoun reflects more accurately than the masculine the biblical God
and urges its use. [16] Johnson's use of the feminine gender is metaphorical:
God, like a woman, is wisdom, spirit, flesh, mother. [17] An increasing
number of books on women's spirituality use *he* for God in solely negative
contexts and *she* for solely positive statements. Thus the deity of an

14. Sallie McFague, *The Body of God: An Ecological Theology* (Minneapolis: Fortress,
1993), 147.

15. See, for example, Starhawk, *The Spiral Dance: The Rebirth of the Ancient
Religion of the Great Goddess* (San Francisco: Harper & Row, 1979).

16. Elizabeth A. Johnson, *She Who Is: The Mystery of God in Feminist Theological
Discourse* (New York: Crossroad, 1992), 242–43.

17. Ibid., 124–87.

uncaring hierarchy is a *he*, while the God of supportive nurture is *she*.[18] Janet Morley is one of few to argue one level deeper, that the feminine pronoun takes on a healthy, albeit disturbing meaning when a woman rails against a distant, uncaring deity newly termed *she*.[19]

Assigning certain human tendencies and personality inclinations to women over against men, however, is a dubious enterprise, especially when women frame the sentence so that the female characteristics are overwhemingly or wholly positive. Contemporary women rightly reject fifteen hundred years of hearing that males are more rational, and thus more godlike, than females. Current claims that women are more wise or more nurturing than men, and thus more godlike, enshrine nineteenth-century conceptions of the cult of true womanhood, which attempted to confine women of the middle and upper classes to the domestic sphere. Much of this use of *she* is intended to raise women's self-esteem by linking them with the divine, but it is questionable whether any truth lies in the claims of females' closer replication of God.

Some Christians use *she* for the Spirit. In Hebrew, the noun *ruah* (spirit) is feminine gender and takes a feminine pronoun. Some mystics and poets retained the idea of a feminine spirit. Perhaps some people believe that the Spirit is literally the feminine, or female, aspect of God. More likely, this is an example of the use of metaphorical gender: the feminine is seen as poetically appropriate for the Spirit of God. Popularizing the Spirit as *she* is, however, no solution. Assigning *he* to two persons of the Trinity and *she* to the third only further entrenches the notion of God's sexuality. The Spirit as *she* is unacceptable not only because God ends up only one-third feminine, but also because God is neither, as modern American English knows them, *he* nor *she*.

Metaphorical use of the divine *she* may well appear in hymnody.[20] Several recent hymns use *she* in describing the eagle's mothering, and then without using any divine pronoun compares the eagle to God.

---

18. An example is Nancy Mairs, *Ordinary Time: Cycles in Marriage, Faith, and Renewal* (Boston: Beacon, 1993), 162–63.

19. Janet Morley, "I Desire Her with My Whole Heart," in *Feminist Theology: A Reader*, ed. Ann Loades (Louisville: Westminster/John Knox Press, 1990), 162.

20. See, for example, Brian Wren, "Who Is She," in *A New Hymnal for Colleges and Schools*, ed. Jeffrey Rowthorn and Russell Schulz-Widmar (New Haven: Yale University Press, 1992), #15, and many other new compositions.

Sophia poems refer to the divine *she*. One assembly, in singing a seventeenth-century hymn with twenty masculine pronouns in its English translation, substituted feminine pronouns in two of the four stanzas; this arbitrary alternation used the two pronouns apart from any gender stereotypes and made clear that neither pronoun is true. But in general, the divine *she* has the unfortunate effect of accentuating the pronoun, surely not the point either of the pronoun or of Christian speech about God.

Fortunately most liturgy talks *to* God rather than about God. Thus in the liturgy God is usually *you*. Some of the problematic areas remaining in Christian liturgy can look to the second-person solution. The English Language Liturgical Consultation, for example, has eliminated the *him* in the Sursum Corda and has proposed translations of the Benedictus and the Magnificat that are cast in the second person, thus eliminating several dozen masculine pronouns from these biblical canticles.[21] This model can serve for the psalter as well. While ancient Hebrew could alternate second and third person with abandon, flipping from God as *you* to God as *he* within a single sentence, such switching grammatical person is not standard American English. Thus casting the psalms in the second person improves them as liturgical texts.

The body of classic hymnody requires massive adaptation in this regard. Many hymns, written originally in other languages, can be retranslated to eliminate masculine pronouns. A genuine effort of this kind might then allow the church to continue to use some hymns in which a superb but archaic English retains masculine pronouns, especially were this body of hymns to be balanced by a new collection that utilized *she*, and not solely in reference to God as the mothering one. In this way, some responsibly framed metaphorical gender could remain in the church's poetry.

But ultimately the final option is best: Christians must abandon use of the third-person pronoun in reference to God. The initial reaction of many people—that such a practice would be impossible—is clearly wrong. A growing number of speakers and writers of the Christian faith have already eliminated the traditional masculine pronouns, and

---

21. English Language Liturgical Consultation, *Praying Together* (Nashville: Abingdon, 1991).

an impressive group of liturgical committees and arbiters of denominational language have advocated and currently practice such usage.
Indeed, many Christians remain unaware of such editorial decisions;
when the prose is carefully framed, the absence of pronouns is not
evident.

Christians have the added question of pronominal reference to Christ.
The Christian belief that God became incarnate in a male human being
has fueled an androcentric bias that occasionally tries to defend masculinity inherent in God. In fact, recent decades have seen an inten-
sification of this pattern. For example, the Vatican's suggestion that a
Roman Catholic priest's role as *alter Christus* requires that the priest be
a male illustrates the ways that androcentric language, ritual, and art
can distort a profound understanding of divinity. In contrast to this
recent proposal, the theologians of the church have always maintained
not that Christ became male, but, as in the new translation proposed
by the English Language Liturgical Consultation, that Christ became
"truly human." The classic formula that "what was not assumed cannot
be redeemed" applies here: To equate God with the man Jesus is to
delete women from the story of salvation.

This is not to deny that Jesus was a first-century Jewish male. Talking
and imaging of the incarnate Christ, however, cannot finally shrink
God into a first-century male. Well-crafted prose can minimize masculine pronouns even in narratives about Jesus and avoid masculine
pronouns altogether when texts focus on Christ's divine nature.[22] Christian theological language has always had to speak of the two natures
of Christ with care: for example, while Christians affirm that Jesus was
God, they do not say that between Jesus' crucifixion and resurrection
God was dead. Theological language must use great care in crafting
the paradoxes of the faith into speech.

If God is neither *he* nor *she*, neither is the devil. Although belief in
a supernatural evil being is not an essential tenet of the faith, Christian
liturgy does refer to the power of evil with the ancient image of Satan.
The questions at baptism, for example, ask the catechumen to renounce
the devil and all "his" empty promises. Western art had a field day
depicting the story of the human fall, sometimes casting the serpent's

22. See, for example, *Lectionary for the Christian People*, ed. Gordon Lathrop and
Gail Ramshaw (New York: Pueblo Publishing Company, 1986, 1987, 1988).

head as male to suggest the seduction of Eve, sometimes as female to suggest that the very source of evil was feminine. A life-sized painted ceramic made in 1515 for a triumphal arch to honor Pope Leo X depicts the serpent's face and hair as identical to Eve's.[23] Christians would be better served by eliminating gender altogether from the personification of evil.

Admittedly, it is easier for a drafting committee to cast English without masculine pronouns than it is for preachers to reorient their vocabulary. Linguists suggest that such change can occur only when a high percentage of prestigious speakers and writers adopt the new procedure.[24] That is, not only articulate feminists, but also bishops, male theologians, prominent speakers, and popular religious writers must abandon the divine *he*. Eliminating the masculine pronoun will help immensely in the catechetical tasks ahead.

Such a change in pronoun usage will both effect and reflect a prior change in consciousness. The adoption of *Ms.* will be sporadic if society continues to categorize women as either single or married.[25] But *Ms.* is gaining in popularity because in many contexts speakers and writers welcome a female title that does not rely on the often unavailable information of a woman's marital status. In the same way, freedom from the divine *he* will come when the arbiters of Christian speech mature beyond a masculine God. A recent study of the Shakers' bisexual language for the divine demonstrated that only after the Shaker communities established a social order attempting gender equality did the religious language of the Shakers evidence gender-balanced language for God.[26] People who imagine God to be masculine are not likely to purge their language of *he*, while people who believe that *he* belittles God find linguistic reform a welcome challenge.

23. The ceramic from the workshop of Giovanni della Robbia is on display at the Walters Art Gallery in Baltimore.

24. Nancy M. Henley, "This New Species that Seeks a New Language," in *Women and Language in Transition*, ed. Joyce Penfield (New York: State University of New York Press, 1987), 19.

25. Robin Lakoff, *Language and Woman's Place* (New York: Harper, 1975), 42.

26. Linda Mercadante, *Gender, Doctrine and God: The Shakers and Contemporary Theology* (Nashville: Abingdon, 1990), 156.

four

IDENTIFYING THE BIBLICAL GOD

Several variants of the thirteenth-century dictum *extra ecclesiam nulla salus* are characteristic of our time. While some Christians maintain that absolutist "There is no salvation outside the church," one hears also "There is no salvation," "There is salvation in any and every religion," even "There is surely no salvation within the church." Many American Christians, for whom tolerance in the face of diversity is an extremely high value, find it increasingly difficult to identify their religious tradition as distinct from, and at least in some ways preferable to, other religions. This task of clarification is not new; identifying the biblical God and distinguishing that God from other deities predates even the biblical record. The Scriptures demonstrate three techniques useful for this task of identification: rejection, incorporation, and differentiation.

THE BIBLE AND BIBLICAL MONOTHEISM

Biblical monotheism did not spring fully armed from the head of some Zeus. Contemporary studies of the ancient Near Eastern culture have demonstrated that perhaps for centuries the Israelite clans participated more or less in the worship of the Canaanite deities.[1] Furthermore, scholars find historically inaccurate the neat differentiation between an orthodox Israelite faith and the people's popular religion. A more plausible distinction can be drawn between commonplace Israelite religious practices and a reformist bias of later historians and religious

1. Mark S. Smith, *The Early History of God: Yahweh and the Other Deities in Ancient Israel* (San Francisco: Harper & Row, 1990), 1–26.

purists. The monotheistic passion of later purists, however, cannot blind us to considerable evidence of an earlier polytheism, or at least henotheism, in biblical culture.

A Pattern of Rejection

One lane in the roadway from polytheism to monotheism was characterized by a pattern of rejection. We read of prophetic calls to repudiate worship of Baal, the periodic housecleaning that removed the goddess pole from the temple, and scattered prohibitions of child sacrifice. One such narrative is the famous story in 1 Kings 18 of Elijah's contest with and slaughter of the 450 prophets of Baal and Asherah. Much current scholarship has sought to determine whether especially Asherah, the goddess of life symbolized by a tree or a pole, was repudiated, or whether Baal, as competitor of YHWH, was rejected while Asherah was more or less tolerated.[2] Such repudiation, not content to restrict itself to the weapon of polemical speech, became notorious in Christian history: one thinks of the Crusades, the Conquistadors, and the witch-hunts. Not surprisingly, such a pattern is unpopular in our time. Fortunately the Scriptures themselves model other more accessible patterns.

A Pattern of Incorporation

A second and opposite path toward orthodox Judaism was that of incorporation. Although YHWH was different from the Canaanite deities, the Israelites sometimes used their neighbors' religious language to describe their own deity.[3] In one example of such incorporation, Genesis 14, Abram had successfully defeated a coalition of chieftains to rescue his nephew Lot, and King Melchizedek of Salem praised Abram for his victory. Melchizedek worshiped the high god of the Canaanite pantheon under the title El Elyon, usually translated "God Most High." According to Genesis, Abram responded to Melchizedek by claiming that the Israelite god, YHWH, is God Most High. _God Most High_ becomes one of the designations of the Israelite god, appearing

2. Ibid., 80–99.

3. See, for example, Tryggve N. D. Mettinger, *In Search of God: The Meaning and Message of the Everlasting Names*, trans. Frederick H. Cryer (Philadelphia: Fortress, 1987), 92–98.

especially in the poems in Deuteronomy 32 and 2 Samuel 22 and in the psalter.

A second incorporation is the divine name El Shaddai. Given in Genesis 17 as God's revealed name, El Shaddai was a divine name used by an ancient people in the Transjordan. This divine name occurs in the Pentateuch, Ruth, the Psalms, Isaiah, Ezekiel, Joel, and repeatedly in Job. Recent attention to the etymology of *Shaddai* suggests that the obscure name may derive from the word for mountain, thus connoting the male deity who resides on the high mountain holding up the sky, or may derive from the word for breast, thus recalling the female deity of the twin peaks.[4] But neither male nor female imagery survives in translation. The Septuagint's rendering of this divine name shows the influence of Greek philosophical theology on the translators, for El Shaddai was cast as *Pantokrator*, in English "Almighty." The biblical record is not interested in the word's etymology, however. Rather, as with El Elyon, El Shaddai, previously worshiped by other tribes, is not rejected but incorporated into YHWH of Israel.

More examples exist. In Genesis 16 Hagar praises God as El-Roi, "the God who sees." Scholars take this title to be the name of the deity worshiped at the well that is the site of the narrative. In Genesis 21, Abraham calls on YHWH as El-Olam, "God Everlasting," the title of El used in worship at Beer-sheba. Jacob's vision of angels in Genesis 28 occurs at El's shrine at Bethel, and in Genesis 31 the angel of God names YHWH as El-Bethel. All these identifications of El—Elyon, Shaddai, Roi, Olam, and Bethel—are absorbed into the Hebrew tradition as appropriate titles of their own tribal deity. An emerging monotheism incorporated previous deities into its own not only supratribal but increasingly cosmic God. Perhaps those deities who are not an active threat to the new religion—for example El, a creator deity far removed from human life—were easily incorporated, while the more popular deities Baal and Asherah, whose cultic devotion was important to the people, had to be rejected.

This pattern demonstrates that humans can speak of the divine only in the language available to them. Religious visionaries stretch the

4. Frank Moore Cross, *Canaanite Myth and Hebrew Epic* (Cambridge, Mass.: Harvard University Press, 1973), 54–55.

available language; religious reformers amend it; theologians trim it; liturgists ritualize it. But finally all are relying more or less on the linguistic categories provided by their speech and culture. As Edward Schillebeeckx has explained, "These authors express this salvation in terms of the world in which they live, their own milieu and their own questions—in short, in terms of their own world of experience."[5] Thus for the Israelites, the titles and imagery of El were deemed the best raw materials to shape into their description of YHWH.

This pattern of appropriating categories from the culture and its religions continues in the Christian Scriptures and can be seen in the Johannine adoption of *Logos*. The idea of the Logos in Greek philosophy was articulated in the sixth century before Christ and became important in later Stoic thought. According to these Greek thinkers, the universe required an ordering principle so that the flux of continuing life might be held together and directed toward a reasonable goal. For some Greeks, Logos was the objective power of reason; for the more religious, it was an aspect of the mind of God. But whether a philosophical concept or a theological category, Logos was fundamental to the universe in much the same way that reasoning ability was accepted as the identifying characteristic of the human species. This concept was part of the world-view and vocabulary of the Greek-speaking Jews who translated the Hebrew Bible into the Septuagint.[6] The recurring phrase in Hebrew "the word of YHWH" was rendered as the *Logos* of the *Kyrios*. At this stage, Logos is an idea, not a being, male or female.

Concurrent with the Greek speculation about the Logos, Jewish poets, stretching their own rules against anthropomorphizing the deity, personified the divine aspect of wisdom. In poems that may have functioned either as metaphoric delights or as a more significant in-corporation of polytheistic imagery, Jewish writers hypostatized divine wisdom, Hokmah, as a goddesslike figure. A heavenly being residing with God, she ordered creation at the beginning of time and con-tinues to guide humankind into truth. The personification of God's wisdom became a verbal icon, at least in the Sophia poems.[7] God's

5. Edward Schillebeeckx, *Interim Report on the Books Jesus and Christ* (New York: Crossroad, 1981), 15.

6. Raymond E. Brown, S.S., *The Gospel According to John*, The Anchor Bible 29 (Garden City, N.Y.: Doubleday, 1966), 1:519–24.

7. See, for example, Roland E. Murphy, O.Carm., *The Tree of Life: An Exploration of Biblical Wisdom Literature* (New York: Doubleday, 1990).

presence, the Shekinah, was another divine quality hypostatized in Hebrew poetry.

The Johannine community applied this Jewish skill of personifying a divine quality to the Greek category of Logos. Some scholars maintain that John 1 is based on an earlier pre-Christian praise of Logos.[8] Christ is described as the Logos of God, who in the person of Jesus incarnated the mind of God in the world. This Christ is intimately related to God from eternity and guides the entire universe. Through the ordering of chaos, Christ reveals the divine will. These ascriptions to Christ have merged the Hebrew Hokmah with the Greek Logos, the female aspect of the image being jettisoned by Jesus' maleness. Logos Christology became important for the pre-Nicene theologians, who described Jesus Christ as the preexistent image of the divine, the revelation of the divine will, the rational power of the universe, the personification of the mind of God.[9]

In post-Nicene times, Logos language declined in importance, because orthodox theologians judged that it too easily led to subordinationism, the heresy that the second person of the Trinity was subordinate to the first. The Greek ideal of Logos involved emanation, for the Logos proceeds from the mouth of God, and this could be taken to demonstrate Christ's secondary status. Thus orthodox theologians came to rely on the language of "the eternally begotten Son of the Father" as, in their view, less prone to misinterpretation, more likely pointing to the equality of the first and second persons of the Trinity.

From the vantage point of the twentieth century, the orthodox strategy to keep the second person equal with the first appears to have failed. The intention, to raise the incarnate Christ to God, ironically resulted in the opposite: God was demoted to the level of a man. Christian theologians were probably unconscious to what great degree they incorporated the concept of Logos into the name Son. One reason *Son* language does not successfully convey its orthodox theological meaning is that contemporary Christians do not know Logos philosophy.

8. Brown, *The Gospel According to John*, 1:19–21.

9. C. H. Dodd, *The Interpretation of the Fourth Gospel* (Cambridge, England: Cambridge University Press, 1968), 276–79; J. N. D. Kelly, *Early Christian Doctrines* (New York: Harper & Row, 1958), 95–101; and G. L. Prestige, *God in Patristic Thought* (London: SPCK, 1956), 116–28.

Son incorporates *Logos*, just as praise to God as Sophia incorporated goddess veneration. The ideas of El Shaddai and Logos remain embedded in the roots of imagery that flower later in history. Those who wish to proclaim a unique religious experience envision that experience in the religious categories or philosophical concepts of their own culture. They adopt and adapt the contemporary category, and consciously or unconsciously, their vision is molded by the preexisting meanings of the chosen categories. A later consensus may decide that the cultural categories led the unique religious vision astray, and the tradition attempts to drop the cultural baggage along the wayside. But in fact the religious vision has already been altered to some degree by the decades or centuries of usage. To some degree, the alien idea has been incorporated.

A Pattern of Differentiation

A third biblical pattern is differentiation. In this pattern a prepositional phrase qualifies a more general name or title of the deity, to differentiate without polemic the believers' God from other deities. The phrase "the God of our fathers" is one example of differentiation. The fathers may be named: Abraham, Isaac, Jacob, Israel. The phrase may be individual, as in "my fathers," or communal, as in "our fathers."[10] Despite the narratives in which Sarah, Rebekah, Leah, and Rachel are prominent figures who exercise power and effect its transfer, the codifiers of the tradition thought patriarchally: the Hebrew deity is designated the God of Abraham, never the God of Sarah, nor (a phrase to modern liking) the God of Abraham and Sarah. The writers see the clan as rooted in one's patriarch, and thus one's God is identified by that patrilinear line.

In many primary societies, deities were thought to reside in the land or in the sky directly above the land. Divine action was identified with the weather or the fertility of a certain locale, and the people appealed to the divinity with demonstrated competence in that area of the world. For the biblical people who recalled a nomadic past, however, God was identified not primarily with the created order, with soil and rain, but with tribal history by means of a covenant relationship with the people. When Israel was taken into exile, the monotheistic prophets

10. Mettinger, *In Search of God*, 53–65.

confidently proclaimed that because their deity rises high above earth, YHWH was still their Savior in a distant land.

Both the Jewish and the Christian traditions have developed significant theological ideas from phrases like "the God of our fathers." That God attends more to males than to females has been an inference assumed, albeit sometimes denied. But more positive theological ideas evolved. Christianity understands God to be one who travels with humanity; who is beyond land and sky, space and time; whose relevation has come to specific historical people; whose power is seen not so much in a stroke of lightning as in the turns of human affairs; whose covenant extends from the past into the future. People who genuinely depend on the cycles of nature for their existence experience nature not as romantically charming but as sometimes brutally uncaring. In contrast, the biblical God is other than nature, and God's salvation is seen in events far more surprising than the coming of spring.

This pattern of differentiation continues in the Christian Scriptures. As those Jews who accepted that Jesus of Nazareth was the Messiah distinguished themselves from those who did not, the central question of Christian identity became that which Jesus posed to his disciples: "Who do you say that I am?" By extension, Who is God in relation to Christ?[11] Christian language had to differentiate itself from Jewish speech, Greco-Roman polytheism, and Hellenistic philosophical deism. That Christians pray "in the name of Jesus" means not that each prayer must include this tag line, but that the God Christians worship is the one Christians know in the life and death of Jesus. "The God of our fathers," that is, the deity claimed by the Hebrew tradition, became for the early Christians "the God and father of Jesus Christ." So it is that those people who worship "the God of their fathers" are known by their family name the Jews, while those who worship "the God and father of Jesus Christ" are named by the honorific of that Jesus, Christians. Use of the image of fatherhood dramatically increased during the early church until it dominated the language that described the identity of Jesus.[12] "Who do you say that Jesus is?" The church answered, "The son of God." By extension, God became "the father of Jesus Christ."

11. Robert W. Jenson, *The Triune Identity: God According to the Gospel* (Philadelphia: Fortress, 1982), xii, 8.

12. See chap. 7 for a discussion of father language.

It is often the case that people who begin as Christians and eventually find themselves outside the church, whether by choice or expulsion, during their life or after the course of time, are usually those whose Christology is too far afield. That the Shakers in honoring Ann Lee made her equal to Jesus moved them to the farthest periphery of the faith.[13] That Thomas Jefferson's editing of the Christian Scriptures omitted all miracles and the resurrection itself demonstrated his Enlightenment deism.[14] In our time feminists and womanists must grapple with Christology.[15] "Who do you say that I am?" remains the differentiating criterion in marking language that is distinctively Christian.

Such differentiation is a necessary task in religion, for there is no future for religion-in-general. If spirit and power exist in the universe beyond the individual's limited spirit and power, it follows that where that spirit is, how it functions, and the person's ability to access it are matters of extreme importance. The world's religions, addressing the same questions, offer a great variety of radically contradictory answers.[16] Each religion must define itself: these, a religious tradition says, constitute our answers to the world's religious questions. According to our deepest wisdom, here, and not there, is sacred power; this way, and not that, is how we can access that power. To avoid any differentiation is finally suicidal to religion itself, for it is only within specific religious traditions that the universal religious questions escape banalities to reach more deeply and sharply toward truth and compassion. That each religious group should study and seek to understand other religions is a growing necessity in a crowded world. The proposal that religions are essentially the same with interchangeable parts, however, is an ignorant notion, unsupportable by serious examination.

13. Robley Edward Whitson, ed., *The Shakers: Two Centuries of Spiritual Reflection* (New York: Paulist, 1981), 48, passim.

14. Thomas Jefferson, ed., *The Jefferson Bible* (New York: Grosset & Dunlap, 1940).

15. See, for example, Patricia Wilson-Kastner, *Faith, Feminism and the Christ* (Philadelphia: Fortress, 1983), and Jacquelyn Grant, *White Women's Christ and Black Women's Jesus: Feminist Christology and Womanist Response* (Atlanta: Scholars Press, 1989).

16. See Roy A. Clouser, *The Myth of Religious Neutrality* (Notre Dame, Ind.: University of Notre Dame Press, 1991), 9–48, for a discussion of the incompatible worldviews of different religions.

GOD AS CREATOR

The biblical principles of rejection, incorporation, and differentiation continue to guide the church in formulating Christian prayer. The church uses and amends the categories and language of its culture to speak its faith. It is not easy to keep the balance: one branch of the church may be more interested in incorporation, another more dedicated to differentiation. One decade may find the society fascinated with inclusion, a later decade with distinctions. These principles are continuously at work in the current consideration of God as creator.

It is common for polytheisms to postulate one of the deities as creator. In some religions, the creator deity is no longer active in the universe; creation is completed, and other deities are ascendant. The Canaanite creator El received far less devotion than the socially active Baal. The ancient Israelites incorporated the language of El as maker of heaven and earth into their praise of YHWH. The Scriptures include several quite different stories of YHWH creating the world. In the mythological Psalm 104, God is clothed in light, stretches out the sky like a tent, builds the world's foundations, and talks to the seas. In Genesis 2, a highly anthropomorphized picture of God attending to human civilization, not the universe but the primordial family is formed by God's artistic attempts. Genesis 1 is the Bible's most intellectually sophisticated creation story, in which a transcendent omnipotent deity creates the universe in a logical order, moving from simplicity toward greater complexity as the week proceeds.

Rather than describing creation as the artistic design of a skilled deity, Israel's Babylonian neighbors imagined the universe as the residue of an ancient battle. The victorious male Marduk, after tearing apart the body of the female sea monster Tiamat, reuses her corpse as the matter of the universe.[17] This Babylonian tale of a primeval battle between the sky deity and the sea monster is given only a passing reference in Psalm 74 and did not become important in biblical memory. Repudiation of this imagery implied that according to Hebrew religious sensibility, armed conflict is not inevitable in human life, as if proceeding unavoidably from the deity's original struggles. A vestige of the primordial sexual contest remains, however, in the story of Eve's

---

17. "The Enuma Elish," in Barbara C. Sproul, *Primal Myth: Creating the World* (San Francisco: Harper & Row, 1979), 91–113.

condemnation, and evil was repeatedly envisioned in female form throughout the Jewish and Christian traditions. Battle imagery survived in the Hebrew tradition by being historicized: the enemy was not the primordial sea monster, but Pharaoh's army. [18] Battle imagery remained in the legend of Michael and Lucifer and moved to the future through apocalypticism. Christianity kept the battle language but shifted it off creation.

The apostolic fathers sanctioned language about God as creator to combat cultural ideas that a lesser and perhaps pernicious deity formed the world, and the church gave this divine title top billing in the creeds. [19] The idea of creation *ex nihilo* has occupied Christian theologians, and even into recent times theologians used Genesis 2 as the proof they sought of an androcentric universe and church. But the primary truth taught from the creation stories has been the sovereignty of a transcendent and beneficent God: God is other than the universe, and the universe created by God is good. In an age when many Christians accept scientific theories about evolution and when resurgent pantheism claims that the universe in itself is divine, the creation story proclaims that God is not only within, but also other than, prior to, and beyond the universe.

God as creator of the universe was less important to Jews and Christians than was God as the creator of the people. Here we see the principle of differentiation at work. Second Isaiah articulates the theologically central idea that God is the creator of Israel; that after the universe was formed, Israel was formed and saved, and that this second creation is the more important to narrate and celebrate. The female image of God in labor pains in Isaiah 42 is applied not to the created universe, but to the redeemed people. For Jews, the exodus is the primary creation story. Incorporating this same theological idea, Christians read Genesis 1 at the Easter Vigil, for in the resurrection the world is created anew.

Many Christians acknowledge that God's creation has not been a sufficient theme in prayer and that the West's maltreatment of creation

18. Gordon W. Lathrop, "A Rebirth of Images," *Worship* 58 (1984): 295.
19. Kelly, *Early Christian Doctrines*, 83–87.

has been (and ought to be) the subject of vociferous criticism.[20] The suggestion in Genesis 1 that God gave the universe to human beings to meet their own needs has been used as warrant to value creation only in terms of its use by human civilization. To learn more respect for God's creation, churches are now looking to other religious traditions—for example, some Native American peoples—to inspire new language for prayer. But careful study of Native American spiritualities demonstrates great varieties of belief, and Christians need to think before they borrow and edit.

Some Christians have adapted the prayers of the Lakota Sioux shaman Black Elk for liturgical use.[21] Distinction is needed, however, even among Black Elk's prayers. The records of Black Elk's life indicate a stark contrast between the shaman's great vision of 1871 and the imagery of the Ghost Dance twenty years later. The earlier Lakota conception saw the natural world alive with sacred power, with "Six Grandfathers" being Black Elk's relational language to bind together north, south, west, east, earth, and sky.[22] Black Elk's pantheistic ritual honors the earth because the earth itself contains the power humans must access: the earth is divine. But as Christians continued to evangelize the natives with biblical speech and the American government sought to destroy the native religion, the natives' religious imagery changed. In the messianic Ghost Dance, the tribes anticipated the arrival of the son of the Great Spirit who would destroy the world's systemic evil and create a new perfected order.[23] Black Elk's belief in sacred power within nature that all creatures can access surrendered to an apocalyptic monotheism of a despairing people. Christians searching Native American ritual for language need to differentiate: the young Black Elk is not praising God, and the Christian singing Psalm 104 is not ingesting the divine

---

20. See the recent ecological theology in Sallie McFague, *The Body of God: An Ecological Theology* (Minneapolis: Fortress, 1993), and Rosemary Radford Ruether, *Gaia and God: An Ecofeminist Theology of Earth Healing* (San Francisco: HarperCollins, 1992).

21. See, for example, worship materials for the World Day of Prayer, March 6, 1981 (New York: Church Women United, 1980), and for World Community Day, November 1992 (New York: Church Women United, 1991).

22. *Black Elk Speaks*, ed. John G. Neihardt (Lincoln: University of Nebraska Press, 1961), 25–30.

23. Ibid., 232–37.

power of nature. Prayers ought to be accurate expressions of religious belief, but they can also be incongruous, multicultural playacting with little regard to meaning and a cavalier attitude toward other traditions.

GOD AS SOPHIA

A second example of such differentiation of the creator image occurs in the Sophia poems, in which divine wisdom, metaphorically pictured as the wise woman of the skies, climaxes the creation of the world with the creation of the law.[24] The image of Lady Wisdom has received so much attention recently that it calls for our particular consideration. The Jewish wisdom literature, Proverbs, Baruch, Sirach, and Wisdom, contains poems in which divine wisdom is personified as a woman. In some poems she is like a wise woman in the community advising human behavior; in later poems she bears in herself divine powers of creation, preservation, and the maintenance of justice; finally she is the primary Neoplatonic emanation of divinity. Considerable scholarly discussion has addressed the origin and meaning of this metaphor. How much were the Israelites influenced by the wisdom goddesses of their neighbors? Is Hokmah an Israelite form of the Egyptian Maat? Was Sophia, like Asherah, an actual goddess worshiped by other-than-orthodox Jews? More consensus exists about Sophia's fate in Christianity. Since *wisdom* is a feminine noun in both Hebrew and Greek, the parallel idea of God's word, *logos,* which is a masculine noun in Greek, was a more convenient metaphor for application to Jesus. In Christianity Lady Wisdom goes into hiding, replaced by a gender-neutral wisdom as an attribute of Christ, or, in medieval times, reappearing as a metaphor for Mary.

An impressive list of Christian contemporary reformers believe that the metaphor of Sophia has the potential to establish itself as a significant, if not indeed the primary, description of God.[25] But many questions present themselves. Historically, in the wisdom literature,

24. See Pheme Perkins, "Sophia and the Mother-Father: The Gnostic Goddess," in *The Book of the Goddess Past and Present: An Introduction to Her Religion,* ed. Carl Olson (New York: Crossroad, 1983), 97–109.

25. See, for example, Elizabeth A. Johnson, *She Who Is: The Mystery of God in Feminist Theological Discourse* (New York: Crossroad, 1992), 124–87, and Susan Cady, Marian Ronan, and Hal Taussig, *Wisdom's Feast: Sophia in Study and Celebration* (San Francisco: Harper & Row, 1989).

the female image was a male projection into the skies of a value their androcentric culture reserved for men. That is, those who lauded Sophia were male sages, who while personifying the Torah as female attempted to restrict its study to males. One is reminded that a culture which honors a goddess does not necessarily honor women.[26] In fact, some historians suggest that androcentric cultures honor a feminine ideal as one technique, perhaps unconscious, to compensate for their disregard for women. For example, it was as the intertestamental literature became more misogynist that Sophia gained in ascendancy.[27] Contemporary Christians need to be conscious of this historical pattern and stay alert to the possibility of its recurrence. It is intriguing that the recent hymn text "Who Comes from God," a praise of "Great Sophia," has been written for the Marian tune *Salve Regina Coelitum*.[28] Serious attention to the causes and meanings of Marian devotion are required before Marian descriptions are appropriated for God.

A second consideration is that there is no particular truth in wisdom being female. Some men are wise, some women are wise. That a culture may grant women a much longer life or much more occasion than men to gain interior wisdom is hardly a situation to be emulated. It is illogical for contemporary Christians to reintroduce an archaic wisdom goddess while simultaneously denying that human qualities and personality tendencies such as rationality or wisdom are gender-specific.

A third consideration for the church is how well this religious divine language conveys divine mercy. It is insufficient to provide biblical proof texts for the church's use of the image. Since vastly more biblical examples exist of the divine male than of the divine female, such

---

26. See, for example, Marina Warner, *Alone of All Her Sex: The Myth and the Cult of the Virgin Mary* (New York: Knopf, 1976), 335–39. Serge Schmemann reported that resurgent religion in Russia includes a Christian Marian center, Bogorodechnyi (Mother of God), which "worships the Virgin Mary and preaches hatred for all women—especially mothers—who do not repent and join the organization." "Religion Returns to Russia, with a Vengeance," *The New York Times* (28 July 1993): A8.

27. Julie Bevenour, "Women's Role in the Book of Sirach," student paper, La Salle University, 1992.

28. Patrick Michaels, "Who Comes from God?" in *NewSong* 4 (September 1991). The connection between Sophia and Mary is made explicit in Gail Paterson Corrington, *Her Image of Salvation: Female Saviors and Formative Christianity* (Louisville: Westminster/John Knox Press, 1992), 170–72.

fundamentalism will finally not serve the church well. Rather, Christians need to show how Sophia can speak the gospel. In the Hebrew poetic conceits, wisdom is the power of the created order. To grasp wisdom is to understand the universe and to live by its rhythm. Some poems suggest that the chosen people have more access to wisdom than do their neighbors, but these poems are marked more by national chauvinism than by the surprise of divine mercy.

The church is instructed by the patterns of its tradition. Ought Christians incorporate Sophia into their image of God? Absolutely: the image can enhance praise of God's creative wisdom; it can help Christians live within the structures of the created order; it provides a female metaphor. The "O" antiphons of Advent present Wisdom as one of seven metaphors of the coming one; in many churches, the readings of the Easter Vigil include Lady Wisdom as an image of the resurrection. In cycle B of the three-year lectionary, Sophia is likened to the Christ of John 6, feeding the hungry and personifying a divine wisdom that both surprises and disappoints; for Jesus, refusing to be acclaimed the people's king, eludes the worshiper's grasp, as does the Wise Woman. Much more use of this ancient image is possible. Christian prayer, however, would have to differentiate its image of divinity from that of an ancient goddess whose wisdom is the created order and should nuance the Jewish idea that humans are to live by the law of God's universe. Sophia must come to stand at the foot of the cross.

Christian prayer addresses God as creator, the power not only within but also other than and behind the universe, the good greater than any evil; praises God for divine wisdom permeating the universe and guiding the community; and, as the newly created community, turns that praise into meticulous care for the earth and its people. Yet this Christian language is different from creation language in other of the world's religions. Pantheists see divinity as residing in the earth itself; only as humans are connected to the creativity of the earth are we empowered to live. Goddess worshipers see female power as constitutive of the universe and suggest that especially women can find in themselves the wisdom to live. To such religious ideas Christians listen respectfully and (one hopes) respond intelligently and devoutly. Incorporation, yes; differentiation, yes: the task of identifying the God of Christians goes on.

five

THE ENIGMATIC NAME OF GOD

Does God have a name? Despite what the second-century Christian apologist Justin wrote, "No one can utter the name of the ineffable God: and any one who dares to say that there is a name raves with a hopeless madness,"[1] considerable contemporary discussion concerns what God's name is. What does the current debate mean by "the name of God"? If God has a name, can we say it in English? In English-language Bibles the Hebrew divine name came to be rendered LORD and Jesus came to be titled Lord. This double term LORD/Lord is shorthand for a fundamental formula of Christian faith: Jesus is titled with the name of God. The Nicene Creed uses this term also for the Spirit, who is "the Lord, the giver of life." But this word is both archaic and androcentric. A review of the history of this double term will help us examine proposals for optional translations of this key Christian term.

THE BIBLICAL PICTURE

Quite unlike a later scientific worldview in which a name is an arbitrary label, the ancients saw a name as a quasi-magical key to being. To know something's name was to know its use and perhaps to control that use. In Genesis 2 the first man named all the animals, thus establishing his authority over them. A name also expressed one's identity; thus a life change was symbolized by a name change. Jacob is given the name Israel, Saul takes on the name Paul. The question of what should be the surname of a married woman is a contemporary

1. Justin, "The First Apology," in *The Ante-Nicene Fathers*, ed. Alexander Roberts and James Donaldson (Grand Rapids: Eerdmans, 1979), 1:183.

instance of a name expressing identity and indicating control. For the ancient Hebrews, the name of God is no trivial or academic concern. To call on the deity's name is to invoke that god's very self and to have access to the power of the universe. The Hebrew Scriptures make clear that religious affiliation begins in invoking the proper divine name and that religious purity lies in invoking the divine name properly.

Scholars have discovered that the tetragrammaton, the four consonants YHWH, was a divine name used among tribal peoples in the eastern Sinai prior to 1300 B.C.E.[2] Probably the suggestions in Genesis of earlier Israelite devotion to YHWH are anachronistic. Most likely, the Israelite tribes adapted this divine name from some neighbors about the time of Moses. The central biblical narrative of the revelation of this divine name is that of Moses at the burning bush. Granting a henotheistic world, Moses asked the name of the mighty deity speaking out of the mysterious fire. In the voluminous analysis of the Hebrew in this passage and its most accurate translation, a majority of scholars concur that God's answer is "I am who I am" (Exod. 3:14) and that the "name" of this God (v. 15), borrowed from a neighbor, came to be understood as *the one who is*, a third-person causative form of the verb *to be*. Thomas Aquinas judged *the One Who Is* the most appropriate name of God because the name refers to the ultimate Being that is divinity.[3]

Some scholars propose that the oldest form of the divine name required an object for the verb *to be*: YHWH Sabaoth, meaning "he who is enthroned on the cherubim" or "he who is causes to be the heavenly armies."[4] Whether or not the original users of this divine name understood the deity to be warlike, we know that YHWH quickly absorbed the imagery of Baal, the leader of conquering armies.[5] Perhaps this connection with military leadership led to the choice of *Adonai* as the pious circumlocution for the divine name, which in time only the

2. Tryggve N. D. Mettinger, *In Search of God: The Meaning and Message of the Everlasting Names*, trans. Frederick H. Cryer (Philadelphia: Fortress, 1987), 24–28.

3. Thomas Aquinas, *Summa Theologiae*, 1a.13.11.

4. E. Theodore Mullen Jr., *The Assembly of the Gods*, Harvard Semitic Monographs 24 (Chico, Calif.: Scholars Press, 1980), 187–88.

5. Mark S. Smith, *The Early History of God: Yahweh and the Other Deities in Ancient Israel* (San Francisco: Harper & Row, 1990), 49.

high priest could pronounce once a year. The pious Jew, seeing the four sacred consonants in the biblical text, read aloud *Adonai*, meaning master or lord, a term for male authority. Matthew used a similar circumlocution when writing about the kingdom "of heaven" and the right hand "of Power." When the Jews translated their scriptures into Greek, they rendered the tetragrammaton with the word *Kyrios*, used by the culture to denote respect for any male authority from a stranger to the emperor.

In the Christian Scriptures, *Kyrios* occurs in its full range of meanings. In some passages *Kyrios* can be translated "Sir": Mary Magdalene says to the one she thinks to be the gardener, "Sir, . . . tell me where you have laid him" (John 20:15). In other sentences *Kyrios* is translated to signify the resurrected redeemer: to the disciples Mary Magdalene says, "I have seen the Lord" (John 20:18). The multivalence of *Kyrios* allows Christians to translate John 20 as the story marking Mary Magdalene's discovery of the resurrection. The primitive Christian hymn in Philippians 2 climaxes by acclaiming Jesus as Lord. Here *Kyrios* is the highest divine title possible, conferring divine status on the resurrected Jesus.

Two scriptural passages can be cited to illustrate the linguistic circle of LORD/Lord. Psalm 110 opens with a conversation between God and Israel's king, whom the Hebrew calls "YHWH" and "my *Adonai*," respectively. The classic translation in English is, "The LORD says to my lord." The psalm affirms God's empowerment of the king, who sits symbolically at God's right hand. In Acts 2, Peter's Pentecost sermon cites Psalm 110 as referring not to the dead David but to the resurrected Christ. Peter states that God has raised the Lord Jesus to divine power at God's right hand. The citation in Acts is in Greek and, like the Septuagint's rendering of Psalm 110, reads "*Kyrios* said to my *Kyriō*." The original Hebrew distinguishes between the divine name and the kingly title, but in Greek the distinction gives way to the christological double term.

A different but parallel pattern is evident in the Gospel of John. Greek-speaking people would be accustomed to *Kyrios* as the circumlocution for YHWH, but those with Jewish background would have recognized Jesus' language of "I AM" as a divine claim. When Jesus said, "Before Abraham was, I am" (John 8:58), the Judeans picked up stones to throw at him, because he had taken upon himself the divine name.[6] When in John 18 the soldiers came to arrest Jesus, Jesus responded, *"Ego eimi."* Usually translated "I am he," the phrase is better rendered "Here I AM," for inasmuch as the soldiers respond by falling back to the ground, the author means to indicate that Jesus has spoken the divine name. Although using *Ego eimi*/I AM rather than *Kyrios*/ Lord, the Fourth Gospel also finds a linguistic way to grant Jesus the name of God.

THE TRADITION OF TRANSLATION

The linguistic capability of at least Greek-speaking Jews to use the same word both to substitute for the name of God and to acclaim the status of Jesus influenced biblical translation in many languages, including English. In the Anglo-Saxon language, many words were constructed by attaching two simpler words. An example was the term for the male authority: *hlaford* was derived from *hlaf*, loaf, and *weard*, ward. The authority figure was the one obligated to provide food and protection for the small community he led. This word was chosen by Christian translators to render the *Dominus* of their Latin text. By Middle English, the word was elided into the present *lord*. Not until the Middle Ages did the word *lord* acquire its present connotation of feudal power. The American Revolution added the pejorative connotation of civic injustice.

The development and meaning of LORD/Lord exemplifies an uncomfortable truth: language precedes theology. A specific language makes possible certain theological formulations. That *Kyrios* could function in its multivalent way allowed for Christology to develop as we know it. Christian theological development would have been different had Aramaic rather than Greek been the primitive Christian written language. It is as if the facts of language demonstrate the incarnation. Christianity asserts that God enters human history in particular ways at specific times. To be incarnate is to take on certain flesh: an example of this incarnate particularity is the embodiment of religious expression into certain languages, doxology formed by the specific grammar of a particular age.

6. See Raymond E. Brown, S.S., *The Gospel According to John*, The Anchor Bible 29 (Garden City, N.Y.: Doubleday, 1966), 1:533-38, for an analysis of the *Ego eimi* passages in John.

Because language precedes theology, and because language is continuously changing and developing, theology must always find new ways to speak the gospel. Systematic theology must be perpetually rewritten in the vernacular and by means of current philosophy; otherwise theology ossifies in archaisms. Orthodox Judaism requires ancient Hebrew: the vernacular is not finally significant, because it is not essential. In Christianity, however, the vernacular is essential. It does little good to assert that because the word *hlaford* meant loaf-provider twelve hundred years ago, and since loaf-provider is a wholesome notion, our use of LORD/Lord is secure. LORD/Lord does not mean loaf-provider to speakers of contemporary American English, and it has not meant anything like loaf-provider for centuries. In medieval Europe, the lord was all too often the loaf-consumer, the peasants being the loaf-providers.

The task at hand is to find the existing contemporary speech that says both the mystery of God's identity and the uniqueness of Jesus' status. For although language precedes theology, theology also precedes language. That is, the Christian tradition precedes modern Western culture and the latest permutations of American English speech, and Christians must continuously search for the new words to say the old faith.

Christians cannot talk about a single undisputed "revealed name of God." The Hebrew Scriptures indicate a long, complex history during which the Israelites adopted and adapted divine names from their neighbors. YHWH was one such adaptation. Its specific linguistic meaning appears to have had little import in the Jewish religious tradition. The priests and prophets do not elaborate on the meaning of I AM. The Gospel of John is the biblical book most theologically interested in the divine name, but John's use of the Greek *Ego eimi* stands oblique to the main Hebrew tradition of YHWH/*Adonai*. It is as if in Christianizing the religious tradition, the Johannine community felt free to recast fundamental Jewish vocabulary.

Several different issues arise regarding the liturgical use of LORD/Lord. Liturgical texts are filled with a typographically undifferentiated usage of *Lord*. It is hoped that Bible readers, knowing the traditional typographical usage of LORD/Lord, can understand the psalm that begins, "The LORD says to my lord." But liturgical texts seldom maintain this typographical distinction. Thus many worshipers may be unclear precisely who the much-invoked Lord is. In the history of transmission the gender neutrality of YHWH and I AM has been lost behind the masculinity of *Lord*, the very circumlocution that allowed Christology to develop as it did. Undoubtedly, benign connotations of *Lord* existed in the past. Still today the British Queen is known as Lord of the Isle of Mann. But for contemporary American Christians, the title has an unclear referent, is androcentric and archaic. It casts divinity as masculine, and it hearkens back to an economic system in which vassals were pawns of the power of the ruling class. Neither of these connotations corresponds to the gospel of mercy that the Scriptures proclaim.

SEVERAL RECENT PROPOSALS

Many Christians find the traditional LORD/Lord perfectly acceptable. As well, a good number of reformers, having struggled with this issue, accept LORD/Lord as the best, if not the only, option. Especially for those with a high Christology, the need to find a single word to say both God's name and Jesus' title has thrown them back to LORD/Lord as the most appropriate rendering. This choice is more defensible, however, in biblical translations that distinguish LORD from Lord than in liturgical materials that do not. While Christian orthodoxy does not require perpetual distinction between the first and second person of the Trinity, spelling the divine name as *Lord* is an inadequate way to render the mysterious *I am who I am*, the eternal and merciful One beyond sex and beyond human categories. Thus at least some Christians keep up the search.

An innovation popularized by the publication of the Jerusalem Bible has been to print out *Yahweh* as the translation of the Hebrew YHWH. This scholarly attempt to get behind the circumlocution has influenced psalm translations and contemporary hymns, in which for the first time in Christian history one comes across *Yahweh* in liturgical texts.[7] This usage is problematic on three counts. First, it wholly disregards the religious sensitivities of pious Jews who deem spelling and pronouncing the divine name blasphemous, and it is shocking that within a generation of the Holocaust Western Christians could adopt a religious

---

7. The Joint Committee on Inclusive Language of the National Conference of Catholic Bishops has said that LORD should serve as the translation of YHWH in lectionaries.

practice with apparently no concern for its religious offense to Jews. Second, this ancient Hebrew term can have little religious meaning to contemporary Christians. To speakers of Hebrew, the name has both linguistic meaning and religious resonance, but to speakers of American English the two foreign-sounding syllables inherited from some long-dead polytheists can convey the God of incarnate mercy only with considerable difficulty. The Christian tendency is always to eschew archaisms for the vernacular.

But finally, for Christians to cast the tetragrammaton as *Yahweh* is to beg the christological question. Primitive Christians saw in Christ the incarnate God, and their vocabulary sought to express this mystery. Rendering the name of God as Yahweh affords Christians no way to articulate their confession of the divinity of Christ. Both halves of the double term LORD/Lord need to be addressed. For this reason, the practice of many current liturgical texts to replace the divine LORD with "God," but to retain Lord if referring to Jesus, is similarly problematic, for it makes the name of God other than the title of Christ. As well, this proposal renders nonsensical those psalm passages that praise "the name of the LORD."

An interesting proposal was made by the committee of the National Council of Churches that edited the Revised Standard Version's inclusive lectionary readings.[8] The committee used "the SOVEREIGN ONE" to render the Hebrew YHWH and "the Sovereign Jesus Christ" to render the christological use of *Kyrios*. The fact that *sovereign* can function as both a noun and an adjective granted the necessary flexibility in different sentence constructions. While some people found this proposal worth sustained consideration, it was not extended into liturgical texts, and users of the lectionary found the rendering too alien. Most decisive was the objection from African American Christians who testified that the title *Lord* was essential to their piety. Indeed, the African American spirituals' tradition makes virtually no distinction between Jesus and God, the result being both an extremely high Christology and a God cast in male language. The combined pressures forced the committee to revert to LORD/Lord in its subsequent work.

8. *An Inclusive-Language Lectionary*, ed. the Inclusive-Language Lectionary Committee, Division of Education and Ministry, National Council of the Churches of Christ in the U.S.A. (Atlanta: John Knox Press, 1984), 10–11.

The supreme importance granted by the black churches to the title *Lord* has contributed to the contentment of white liturgical reformers with LORD/Lord. On this issue the different racial history of whites and blacks is evident. Many white feminists are uneasy submitting under a male title of authority, while many African American womanists are glad to call God, not white people, their lord. The latest generation of womanist scholars, however, is beginning to raise the issue of sexism in God-language.[9] It is difficult to anticipate whether more womanists and the African American community as a whole will come to find male language for the divine inadequate.

A Radical Proposal

It is not clear that contemporary Christians have the will, or American English the way, to replace LORD/Lord with another translation. Surely any such replacement would take a century to effect. A word or phrase must be found (1) that renders the tetragrammaton; (2) that acclaims Jesus' divinity; (3) that is felicitous in both biblical translation and liturgical texts; and (4) that does not have disadvantages exceeding its advantages. While human speech offers no perfect term, the search for better language goes on.

One option lies in the expression *the Living One*. When Moses asked God for an identifying name, God's answer was a play on words concerning being. "I AM" and "I am who I am" are phrases which claim that God's name is none other than God's own living being. God is not known and captured in human terms: God is. "I AM" suggests that the Hebrew people did not need a given name for God, a handle on the deity, for God is beyond such manipulation. Rather, God is active in human lives, and that divine truth identifies God. Although the Israelites chose as their circumlocution a title that emphasized God's authority, a circumlocution more germaine to the story of the burning bush is *the Living One*. God is: God is living in the world, and God's life will release all who are enslaved by death. In the twentieth century, many are bored with God and others doubt any possibility of divinity, because death so absolutely limits their existence. Today *the Living One*

---

9. Kelly Delaine Brown, "Who Do They Say that I Am? A Critical Examination of the Black Christ," Ph.D. diss., Union Theological Seminary, 1988.

captures more essentially than a title of authority the sparks of the burning bush and may symbolize more effectively the life of God.

The acclamation of primitive Christians was that Jesus was risen from the dead. As the living one, Christ is active in the community, dispensing the divine Spirit into the whole world. In the life of the risen one is promise for the life of the world. Usually this faith in the resurrection was expressed in the phrases *Jesus is the Christ* and *Jesus is Lord*. The Easter Vigil uses the phrase *Christ is risen*. The weekly liturgy invokes the risen Christ in the assembly with the recurring phrase *The Lord be with you*. The use of an authority title, Lord, expressses only some of this complex meaning, however. The phrase *Christ is alive* or *Christ is the Living One* both keeps the resurrection always on the Christian's tongue and links the life of Jesus with the life of God. What Mary Magdalene says to the disciples is, "I have seen the Living One."

Replacing LORD/Lord with variants of *the Living One* demonstrates an influence more Johannine than synoptic. Because *Kyrios* can mean Sir, a male authority and the tetragrammaton, Luke-Acts is able to connect the humanity of Jesus with divinity by calling Jesus *Kyrios*. What contemporary American English speakers have lost in this linguistic formula is focus on the mysterious divinity. The Johannine use of "I AM," however, stresses the power of God in the person of Jesus. The Johannine Jesus is not so much a worldly leader of a community, as the incarnation of God now alive through the Spirit. Use of the phrase *the Living One*, like the Johannine literature, stresses the life of God in the contemporary Christian community rather than the leadership of the historic man Jesus.

In biblical translation the tetragrammaton, usually cast as "the LORD," would read "the Living One." The recurring "YHWH El" of the Hebrew Scriptures would be cast as "the Living God." The Christian acclamation, usually rendered as "Jesus is Lord," would read "Jesus is the Living One." Variants would be "Jesus lives" or "Christ is alive." The phrase *the Living One* allows acclamation of the resurrection with the same words used to affirm the reality of God, and the fact that the phrase can be adapted to nouns, adjectives, and verbs allows the necessary flexibility for translation of Hebrew and Greek texts.

The repeated use of *Lord* in liturgical texts is a complex issue. According to classical liturgical theology, the assembled community addresses God, not generally Jesus Christ or the Spirit of Christ. Texts like the Agnus Dei or Pentecost hymns were popular devotions, exceptions to the theological pattern, which came to be incorporated into the liturgy.[10] Sometimes the word *Lord* means unequivocally the full Godhead, a title for the deity of creation and salvation. But the neat formula that Christians pray to the Father through the Son in the Spirit does not hold up under close scrutiny of the liturgy itself. In the Sanctus, the Lord is God almighty, and in the Sursum Corda, we give thanks to "the Lord our God." Yet in the Kyrie the title *Lord* alternates with *Christ*, and the recurring "The Lord be with you" means by recalling Easter day to invoke the presence of the Risen Christ in the Sunday assembly. The refrain of many intercessory prayers includes the title *Lord*; and although some Christians understand that the prayer is addressed to God, the Taize community (among others) has popularized intercessory prayers directed specifically to Jesus.[11] Meanwhile the Nicene Creed denotes not the first but the second and the third persons as the Lord. Perhaps this overlapping and interweaving of the title LORD/Lord is inevitable. Some Christians view it as beneficial, even necessary. But to those for whom *Lord* is problematic, both archaic and sexist, its centrality in liturgical texts is unfortunate.

Were LORD/Lord at least sometimes to give way to an alternate translation, the richness of diversity would occur, and perhaps the varied nuances of different divine titles would be religiously helpful. Narratives of Jesus' ministry might cast *Kyrios* as Master, but acclamations of the risen Jesus would praise him as the Living One, just as we praise God as the Living One. The Kyrie might use only "Christ, have mercy,"[12] or could offer such alternates as "God of life, have mercy; Christ our life, have mercy; God of life, have mercy." The Sanctus could be rendered "Holy, holy, holy, Living God of power and might."[13] The *Dominus vobiscum* could be "The peace of Christ be always with you,"[14] thus

10. Joseph Jungmann, S.J., *The Place of Christ in Liturgical Prayer*, trans. A. Peeler, 2d rev. ed. (Staten Island, N.Y.: Alba House, 1965), 144–45, 191–92, 207.

11. See, for example, *Praise in All Our Days: Common Prayer at Taize* (Beds, Great Britain: Faith Press, 1975), 59, 67, passim, and *Praying Together in Word and Song* (Oxford, Great Britain: A. R. Mowbray and Company, 1981), 14–16.

12. See *Supplemental Liturgical Materials*, ed. Standing Liturgical Commission (New York: Church Hymnal Corporation, 1991), 33–34.

13. It is debatable whether the synonyms *power* and *might* are the optimal way to render *Sabaoth*.

14. *Supplemental Liturgical Materials*, 34.

making clear that worshipers are proclaiming the resurrection, not only affirming a divine Inner Light in one another. What some churches call The Lord's Prayer could be titled the Prayer of Jesus, making clear the warrant for Christian continual use of this first-century Jewish prayer.

A radical proposal is not one that a computer can instantly use to replace former terms throughout speech, translations, hymns, and liturgical texts. This proposal is less like replacing *Negro* with *black* than it is like substituting *African American* for *black*. The proposal requires a mental shift, a new way to imagine categories, and as with the term *African American*, calls for considerable discussion as to the ways that the new category is more or less true than the old.

Moderate Proposals

Partial solutions may be an important first step. The dominance of Lord/Lord in liturgical speech can be diminished by using other biblical formulations, such as the term *the Name*. In ancient Israel to invoke the name of God was to appeal for divine power. *The Name* was one of the pious circumlocutions for YHWH. In Genesis 32, Jacob inquired after the name of the mysterious wrestler: he received, in place of the name, a blessing. To invoke the Name is to call on divine mercy.

The gospels indicate that particularly in exorcising demons the disciples invoked the name of Jesus. This is thus a third way, besides Lord/Lord and the Johannine I AM, that the gospels grant divine power to Jesus. To rid themselves of evil, humans invoke the divine name, and for the early Christians, the name of Jesus was that name. In Acts 3 the apostles cure infirmity by invoking the power of the Name. The primitive Christian hymn in Philippians 2 uses the language of "the Name" to indicate the divinity of Jesus. Prayer "in the name of Jesus" implores God to heed the petition, because by sharing the name of Christ the prayer claims access to divine power.

The liturgy could do more with the idea of the Name. Many liturgical acts commence "in the name of" God. Baptism places the Christian under the name of God. Absolution is rendered in God's name. Christians are literally called by "the name," bearing in themselves one of the titles of the one who is named as God. Some churches observe a festival of the holy name of Jesus; however, its placement on New Year's Day destines it in present culture to groggy underuse. Ways could be found to honor the Name in liturgical texts and action, and catechesis can highlight its religious meaning.

The three-year lectionary slights John, and consequently the Johannine I AM has minimal effect on liturgical language. A proposal to appoint exclusively from John the three-year cycle of gospels for Lent and the Fifty Days[15] might give attention to the I AM as one of the biblical ways to equate God's name with Christ's identity. The several hymns that praise "the great I AM" might be sung more often.

The Hasidic tales include this striking story in which an uneducated man confused the punctuation for a full stop with the designation of the divine name:

> Rabbi David of Lelov once heard a simple man who was praying say the name of God after every verse. The reason he did this was that there are two dots one above the other at the close of each verse. The man took each to be the tiny letter Yud or Yod, and since the name of God is sometimes abbreviated in the form of two Yuds, he thought that what he saw at the end of every verse was the name of God. The zaddik instructed him: "Wherever you find two Jews [Yuds] side by side and on a par, there is the name of God. But whenever it looks to you as if one Jew [Yud] were standing above the other, then they are not Jews [Yuds] and it is not the name of God."[16]

Although the rabbi taught that one dot on top of the other was not the designation of God's name, the circumlocution LORD enshrines precisely "one dot above the other," that is, the image of domination as the sign of the divine. The rabbi's instruction should sound familiar to Christians. The two dots must be side by side to denote the divine name; for Christians, baptism into "the name of Jesus" places believers two or three together, side by side with Christ and with one another, and so reveals the powerful mercy of the divine name. It is hoped that use of the titles *the Living One, the Name*, and I AM will diminish the preponderance of LORD/Lord, and that the interplay of these terms can enrich expression of the Christian conviction that in Jesus is the mystery of God.

---

15. Paul Gibson, "The Gospel of John in Lent," paper presented at the North American Academy of Liturgy, Minneapolis, January 2, 1991.

16. Martin Buber, *Tales of the Hasidim: The Later Masters* (New York: Schocken Books, 1948), 185.

six

THE MYTH OF THE CROWN

People of the late twentieth century are ambivalent about myth. Scientific advancements urge us to value cold, hard facts. Schoolchildren learn computer programs rather than memorize poetry. A young clergyman asked, "Now that we know that angels were invented by Assyrian art, how can we sing the Sanctus anymore?" A theological giant in our century, Rudolf Bultmann, maintained that the Bible must be demythologized for its personal existential meaning; he believed that myths were devoid of serious content for modern persons.[1] In some contexts *myth* is a pejorative term, connoting at least ignorance, if not outright deception.

Yet this same culture has lionized Joseph Campbell and embraced his popularization of world myth.[2] Feature films glamorize the mythic worldview of primary societies and castigate more recent philosophy and religion. Hugely popular science fiction and fantasy novels are thinly disguised classic myths in which stereotypical characters contend in the perpetual struggle between good and evil. Sophisticated men attend male retreats and educated women join the Wicca movement: in both, ancient myths of manhood and womanhood are celebrated as life-giving to the contemporary individual and society. It appears that Bultmann was wrong: myth continues to captivate modern people.

1. Rudolf Bultmann, *Jesus Christ and Mythology* (New York: Charles Scribner's Sons, 1958), 17–21.
2. See Joseph Campbell, *The Power of Myth*, with Bill Moyers (New York: Doubleday, 1988), and many other of his publications. See also Lawrence Madden, ed., *The Joseph Campbell Phenomenon: Implications for the Contemporary Church* (Washington, D.C.: Pastoral Press, 1992).

DEFINING MYTH

Philip Wheelwright, in his study of metaphor as tensive language,[3] and Norman Perrin, in his examination of the Bible's royal metaphor,[4] both cite Alan Watt's simple and helpful definition of myth: "Myth is to be defined as a complex of stories—some no doubt fact, and others fantasy—which, for various reasons, human beings regard as demonstrations of the inner meaning of the universe and of human life." Myth is a set of stories, or one long complex narrative. Some myths were a long time, perhaps centuries, in the making. To understand the significance of part of a myth, one must know the entire myth. What elevates any particular narrative to what we call myth is its persuasive and pervasive powers. We are lured into its mythic vision, and its themes recur in human history.

The most formative myths of a culture pervade human thought and behavior. The myth, bolstered by its rituals, serves as a model for living, shaping human consciousness and action according to its own categories of reality. Myths have power to shape consciousness and community no matter what their balance of fact and fantasy. Was Christopher Columbus a hero and saint, or a rogue and plunderer? Even firsthand accounts of Columbus were shaped by the myth of white domination, and so it may be that the old narrative cannot be conveyed in the categories of our time. Yet such a narrative may still have powerful effect: the myth of manifest destiny remains integral to much American identity and foreign policy. When revisionist historians despair of the facticity of the myth, psychologists attest to its power in consciousness. A myth is received as in some way true. As William Faulkner said to explain the inconsistencies in his narratives of the mythic Yoknapatawpha County, "I tell the truth. When I need a fact, I make it up."[5]

The preeminent biblical myth is the myth of the crown. In this hierarchical worldview the natural, social, and religious orders are each a pyramid, the crown of which is the highest intelligence, the great

---

3. Philip Wheelwright, *Metaphor and Reality* (Bloomington: Indiana University Press, 1962), 130.

4. Norman Perrin, *Jesus and the Language of the Kingdom* (Philadelphia: Fortress, 1976), 22.

5. For discussion of William Faulkner's correspondence with his editor, see Frederick R. Karl, *William Faulkner: American Writer* (New York: Weidenfeld & Nicolson, 1989), 118.

purpose, the supreme value, and the base of which supports and serves its crown. The chain of downward supervision and upward obedience holds together natural, social, and religious life. In this formula rests human security, both its salvation and its happiness. This myth undergirds much that is in the Bible. It has shaped Israel's historical memory, the prophets' eschatological hopes, the theologians' description of God and much Christian understanding of Jesus. Christian examples of the myth of the crown exist in doctrinal language, such as the formulation of the Trinity with Father-Son imagery; liturgical language, such as baptismal anointing of heirs of the kingdom; countless hymns;[6] liturgical ritual, such as kneeling in prayer and petitioning God in court speech; and architectural design, such as the eucharistic table evolving into a throne on a dais. No crisis in Christian language is greater than the incongruence of this myth of the crown with modern life. Christians need to reexamine this myth for its ability, both in a democratic society and in the ever-archaic human psyche, to articulate mercy, and consider options for translating its vocabulary into contemporary American English.

TRACING THE MYTH OF THE CROWN

Considerable evidence suggests that many civilizations in the ancient world passed through similar stages of socioeconomic development. A pattern common to many cultures was that when the society enjoyed an excess of food and goods, a successful division of labor, and improved means of communication and transportation, a pyramidal social order arose with a monarch reigning from a central city.[7] Such a society needed more than family stories or nature myths to explain its vast community and to focus its direction. From what did this city-state arise? What was its central focus? What were its goals? The comprehensive myth with its supporting ritual provided the structure for a social order that was too big to see, too complex to grasp.

6. See Brian Wren's *What Language Shall I Borrow? God-Talk in Worship: A Male Response to Feminist Theology* (New York: Crossroad, 1989) for an analysis of what he calls KINGAFAP hymnody, filled with the divine image of King-God-Almighty-Father-Protector.

7. John Wier Perry, *Lord of the Four Quarters: The Mythology of Kingship* (New York: Paulist, 1966), provides examples of this mythic pattern from many civilizations.

According to the common mythic pattern, the original state was one of primeval chaos, potential disaster, actual calamity, or continuous trouble: the difficulty was sometimes objectified as a female monster. The deity, usually male, brought order to the universe and effected happiness in human society by appointing a male ruler, a divine being or the prototype of subsequent kings, who conquered the evil and reigned over a peaceful community. Some myths boast an exciting narrative of a battle and extravagant details of the monarch's majesty. The monarch personified the divine power of good over the evil that always lurks on the edges of human community. The Force reigns supreme, overcoming the evil empire.

In this pattern, the current ruler, usually male, was understood to be descendant from the original monarch who had been enthroned by the deity. The deity had established the monarchy, and the monarch, a "son" of the god, connected the people to the deity. As representative of the deity to the people, the monarch embodied order by enacting laws, upholding justice, personifying discipline, and thereby ensuring continued fertility for the land and the people. As representative of the people to the deity, the monarch interceded for fertility and by a life of integrity brought down divine blessings on the land. With the monarch's palace at the center of the city and the city the *axis mundi*, the people were centered in the beneficence of the deity.

The myth established a pyramidal society. That the deity could bless the monarch and yet affect the whole community required that everything in the society be in its proper place. Centuries before the Platonic articulation of the emanation of being, these societies believed that monarchical power came from above for the purpose of passing life in an orderly manner down through the whole community. Such a society understood itself as a single unit with a united identity and purpose: the rights of the individual were not even contemplated. Stepping outside one's place endangered the entire community. Thus society's offenders were exiled, forced outside of the pyramid that their actions were disrupting. Beyond the walls of the city lay death in the wilderness.

Societies all over the world developed versions of the myth of the crown, and this myth is evident especially in those civilizations prior to and surrounding ancient Israel. In Egypt the pharaoh embodied the male deities Horus, Osiris, and Seth, and orginally was the only human granted eternal life. In Sumer, Babylon, and Assyria, the king was established by the deity as defender of order against chaos. In Babylon, King Marduk was victorious over Tiamat and subsequently founded the city-state. According to Canaanite myth, Baal the lord of human society overcame Yamm, the god of the sea. Ancient Near Eastern iconography contains hundreds of illustrations of these myths, indicating their significance for these peoples.[8]

Although Israel's prophetic tradition did maintain a critical stance toward the monarchy, the ancient Near Eastern myth of the crown forms an essential framework for the Hebrew Scriptures. Originally tribal peoples with diverse backgrounds, Israel came in about 1000 B.C.E. to constitute itself as a nation-state. God, the supreme monarch, was credited with establishing the people as a unit. When warfare threatened the people's survival, it is said that God anointed Saul as the king. The myth of the crown is essential to the memory of the career of David, who established Jerusalem as the central city and personified the cessation of clan warfare. A passage written back into the mouth of Moses (Deut. 17:14-20) describes the ideal king, divinely instituted, whose obedience to God will ensure a wholesome community for all. When contemporary Jews conclude their Passover seder with the phrase, "Next year in Jerusalem!" they are not advocating a vacation in Israel: they are evoking the myth of the crown, the ancient belief that the royal city offers liberty and justice for all.

The myth of the crown is explicitly clear in Psalm 2.[9] The nations threaten chaos, but God, who is known by the title of male authority, has anointed a king in Zion, the ritual hill in the central city. This king, as the son of God, is authorized to protect the people by divine power. The world is to honor both God and the king. In Psalm 47, the royal language is applied especially to God; in Psalm 89, David as the human regent of God reigns over the people. The monarch is afforded the same royal language as God, while also being described as the archetypal human being to whom God relates.

The primary imagery describing Israel's salvation develops from the myth of the crown. When the monarchy weakened, poems called out

8. See Othmar Keel, *The Symbolism of the Biblical World: Ancient Near Eastern Iconography and the Book of Psalms*, trans. Timothy J. Hallett (New York: Crossroad, 1985).

9. See ibid., plates 22, 333, 358, 360, and 406, for iconographic images related to Psalm 2.

for a revival of the Davidic dynasty through the coming of a messiah. In what the intertestamental literature calls the son-of-man, we see yet another permutation of the myth of the crown. Because the messiah tarried and then finally the dynasty was completely obliterated, religious visionaries prayed for the miraculous intervention of another figure, not a descendant of David, but a unique and mighty representative of the people who, similar to the archetypal monarch, would stand between heaven and earth and so link the deity with the suffering people.

The early Christian proclamation recorded in Acts quotes Psalm 2 in claiming that Jesus is the king whom God established as the people's protection against evil enemies (Acts 4:25-26). Jesus is the son of God who receives the promises made to and about David (Acts 13:33-34). The accounts of Jesus' baptism cite language from the myth of the crown: this man, like the king of old, is the anointed king, the son of God. The prolific scholarship in our time focusing on Jesus' parables demonstrates that "the kingdom of God" was the central proclamation of Jesus. Language of kingship is integral to the passion narratives. The imagery of the ascension of Jesus as told in Acts, incongruously important in Christian imagination, is another example of the myth of the crown: Jesus ascends "to sit at the right hand of God," to reign over all with divine authority and to ensure his followers peace and joy.

The epistles contain more language of the kingdom. In some places the myth gets turned upside down: the good news proclaims that the myth of the crown is reworked in Christ and now challenges the status quo. The poor, not the rich on the top of the pyramid, are the heirs of the kingdom (James 2:5). But much Christian use of kingdom imagery suggests, in accord with the ancient myth, that those who are ordered correctly to Christ the king can "enter the kingdom," that is, receive the divine blessings mediated from God through the divine son-king. It is as if despite Jesus' revolutionary witness against the status quo, the myth of the crown, so powerful in imagination and pervasive in speech, shaped the proclamation of the gospel with its ancient values, its pyramidal assumptions, and its triumphalist tone.

CONSIDERING THE MYTH

Although we cannot determine the precise condition of peoples residing under monarchies millennia ago, it is not unreasonable to assume that the crown and its myth accorded the population some good. The city provided companionship, food, shelter, and protection. The root of the word *city*, after all, is the root also of *civilization*. One sees, for example, in the Greek tragedies that the city both literally and symbolically meant social and personal security. The crown's authority could ensure community organization, which lessened individual anxiety and labor. The uncertainty fostered in a nature religion, in which one could never be confident of nature's beneficence, yielded to trust in the deity whose power, personified in the monarch, controlled nature itself. We cannot know how often the myth functioned in this enlightened way, or how often oppression and totalitarianism turned the crown into a nightmare for the people.

The myth of the crown has survived into the twentieth century. Although opinion polls continually inquire into the life of contemporary monarchies, many people who reside in constitutional monarchies speak positively of the crown. It is noteworthy that many biblical scholars writing in English who discuss the biblical myth of the crown in a positive way, claiming that the sovereign is the representative of the people to ensure the stability of the whole, are British or Canadian born.[10] In various places in the world, newly freed nations are considering whether to revive historic monarchies as one step toward social stability. The election process in the United States and the press's daily chronicling of the president's public positions and private life indicate that many Americans fantasize the president as a popularly crowned benevolent monarch with far more political power than current constitutional monarchies afford their heads of state.

Psychologists attest that even when a myth such as that of the crown recedes from one's active consciousness, when these categories retire from daily consideration, the myth continues to function powerfully in the unconscious.[11] That periods of social chaos have led modern people to abdicate their autonomy and to espouse totalitarian rule indicates that the myth of the crown retains its powerful pull on the human imagination. The triangle is a stable structure, and when society

10. For example, Norman Perrin, or Northrop Frye, *The Great Code: The Bible and Literature* (New York: Harcourt Brace Jovanovich, 1982), 87–99.
11. Carl G. Jung, "The Structure of the Psyche," in *The Portable Jung* (New York: Viking, 1971), 28–35.

is rocking and pitching, many people willingly take their ancient place at the base of the pyramid and let the crown take over. The enormous attraction of fundamentalist religion throughout the world in the twentieth century is another demonstration that the myth of the crown remains an archetypal symbol of security and peace.

Whether by accident or unconscious choice, several liturgical reforms of recent decades have increased the church's reliance on the myth of the crown. The much greater use of the psalter throughout American Christianity has revived the myth. Many psalms rely on the myth of the crown as their central image, and these psalms are appointed at those christological festivals, such as Christmas, Epiphany, and Transfiguration, that are especially significant celebrations. The popularity during Advent of iconography of kingship and the innovation of the Reign of Christ Sunday in the three-year lectionary give yet more prominence to this single image of Christ. The church must consider whether, in a century of considerable democratic movement, its increased use of the monarchical myth is psychologically or theologically helpful, or whether the church is once again finding itself in a reactionary stance over against the culture.

Despite the Reign of Christ Sunday, many Americans argue that the myth of the crown is archaic and ought to be jettisoned along with other dead weight.[12] According to this view, the myth is a romanticized throwback to a less enlightened civilization. American democracy rejects the myth of the crown as antediluvian nonsense. Genuine historical research quickly destroys any image we may have imbibed about the glories of monarchies. Any security embodied in ancient monarchies was controlled by the whims of often incompetent, oppressive, and even wicked rulers. According to American historical memory, monarchs served not so much as representatives of the people as manipulators of the poor for their own privileged purposes. Longing for a crown can be seen as infantile behavior. Although the ancient worldview may remain in our unconscious, our educated and reasoned minds reject it absolutely, and any hearkening back to it further obstructs meaningful dialogue between religion and our cultural context.

---

12. For the negative side of Christian use of monarchical imagery, see Sallie McFague, *Models of God: Theology for an Ecological, Nuclear Age* (Philadelphia: Fortress, 1987), 63–69.

Some Christians argue that the Christian faith, by honoring every individual before God, specifically leads away from pyramids. Christianity follows in the prophetic tradition that censured Israel's kings. According to the Magnificat and the Beatitudes, Christ topples monarchs. The gifts of the Holy Spirit are celebrated more clearly in a circle than in a hierarchical pyramid. The myth of the crown arose in ancient society and was adopted by Jews and later Christians only because a more amenable model was unavailable. According to this view, acclaiming Jesus as king is neither religiously meaningful nor theologically profound in our time.

Many feminists suggest that the myth of the crown is irretrievably bound up with sexism.[13] That a man is on top is the common central idea. Read, for example, John Knox's *The First Blast of the Trumpet against the Monstrous Regiment of Women*: his reading of the Bible refused to allow the possibility that a monarch might be female.[14] Thus some Christian feminists see any longing for the crown and manifesting this ancient myth to be reactionary escapes from the difficult but essential Christian task of moving society away from oppressive pyramids toward a circle of baptismal equality for all.

RENDERING THE MYTH

As with every imaginal form of speech that we employ to talk about God, the myth of the crown has limited value. To begin with the obvious, the myth is not factually accurate. God is not enthroned up in the heavens; God's majesty does not literally ensure our safety. Rather, the myth is a human story that, although widely popular throughout the world, is finally only a wish formed into a narrative. How can each of us find peace and security? The individual thinks, perhaps some man greater than I can order my life, represent me before the divine, and convince the deity to attend even to me. It is true that history is filled with examples of the myth enacted. The ancient Hebrews begged Samuel for a king; the Germans in the 1930s gladly elected a Führer. Promising that "they all live happily ever after," the myth attempts to

13. Gerda Lerner, *The Creation of Patriarchy* (New York: Oxford University Press, 1986), 36–53.

14. In *The Political Writings of John Knox*, ed. Marvin A. Breslow (Washington: Folger Books, 1985), 37–78.

effect the security it narrates. Yet the myth remains only a story line, a human hope, an imaginative pattern of longing.

One problem with Christianity's use of the myth of the crown is that while all human speech must be broken in order accurately to describe God,[15] the church tends not to break the royal metaphor. For example, although it is self-evident that when Christians praise God as a rock they know that God is indeed not a rock, the myth of the crown sounds so believable, it is potentially so comforting, that one does not quickly respond, "But of course God is not a king." The creedal understanding of God as the almighty power of the universe seems to find natural expression in the myth of the crown, and messianic language appears to baptize the myth for Christians. That Christ as king was crucified ought to train Christians in myth-breaking. But all too often the myth with its archaic worldview and its sexist assumptions stands unchallenged.

A thoughtless acceptance of the myth of the crown is potentially tragic for Christianity. To the extent that the myth sanctifies male supremacy, it must yield to baptismal equality between the sexes. To the extent that the religious use of the myth reinforces a recurring human tendency to retreat into totalitarianism, it retards the maturing of democracy in the world. To the extent that the myth lays all responsibility for good at the feet of the heavenly monarch, it lessens the urgency with which the church is to shape the world anew by the indwelling of the Spirit. To the extent that the myth lulls Christians into an antiquated worldview or archaic moral prescriptions, it trivializes the profound interaction that must take place between those gifted with God's Spirit and the emerging social situation.

Thus we can begin by listing what the myth of the crown must not be allowed to do. It must not: protect Christians from living reality by the force of its archaism; sanctify patriarchy in the church or the world; short-circuit moral inquiry by means of a romanticized view of the timeless laws passed down from the divine king; or release Christians from the mature human obligation to create a more just society. We need not conclude, however, that the myth must be cremated. Total rejection of the myth would radically diminish the Christian's ability

---

15. Edward Schillebeeckx, *Interim Report on the Books Jesus and Christ* (New York: Crossroad, 1981), 24–25.

to cite the Scriptures. If used correctly and carefully, however, the gospel can build upon and transform the archaic image to speak of God's mercy to the world.

It is essential to realize that Trinity language is rooted in this myth of the crown.[16] The language of Jesus as the son of God comes not from an idea of God's eternal paternity, but from the myth of the crown, which affirms that God as the universe's sovereign appointed a regent to head the human community. Much contemporary debate about the doctrine of the Trinity goes astray because it begins with false assumptions about the trinitarian parental language. While trinitarian language arises from the myth of the crown, however, the best of trinitarian theology developed as a profound corrective to archetypal monarchical language by describing a God not of solitary tyrannical power but of triune interactive love.[17]

For the church to use the myth, the church must find the ways that the myth can speak of mercy. To acclaim God sovereign may indeed be to proclaim mercy. Much contemporary thought begins with the assumption that the individual human being is sovereign. According to American political theory, the people are sovereign. But human beings discover that human sovereignty is marked by agony. This focus on the individual's sovereignty, clearly articulated in the Cartesian statement "I think, therefore I am," must finally acknowledge its shadow side in the Sartrian experience of anguish, forlornness, and despair.[18] The faith that not the human being but God is sovereign and the hope that meaning and direction can arise in something greater than oneself: these are archetypal religious desires. The church may find that the language of God's sovereignty and the locus of that sovereignty in the community can indeed speak faith and hope to people abandoned in the myth of self-sovereignty.

The gospel can teach the church both to speak and to break the myth. If God as the crown of the universe chose to be born in a stable,

16. For a discussion of the roots of Trinity language in the myth of the crown, see chap. 7.

17. For the positive potential for trinitanian theology to correct the myth of the crown, see Catherine Mowry LaCugna, *God for Us: The Trinity and Christian Life* (San Francisco: HarperCollins, 1991), 383–88.

18. Jean-Paul Sartre, *Existentialism and Human Emotions* (New York: Citadel Press, 1957), 18–31.

the myth of the crown has been radically revised. The crown is now on the serving maid. The Oxford Movement parishes in nineteenth-century England attempted with their elaborate ritual to honor poor beggars as if they were royalty:

> A poor woman and her two children were baptized during the Eucharist. All the clergy and all the choir made a procession to and stood round the Font. We could not have done more honour to the Queen's children and their sponsors, but we did not put to shame the tattered rags and mean appearance of these poor people. . . . I never witnessed one of the powers of the church more forcibly—that of raising up the poor. And by inference I felt another of the powers—that of pulling down the rich.[19]

What if the church were to proclaim the crown by boldly, in all its affairs, crowning the poor and the dispossessed? Small movements within the Christian church have undertaken radical challenges to society's pyramidal assumptions. But too often the main branches of the church have gladly relegated such experiments to the twigs. The church has hardly begun to proclaim the Christianized myth of the crown.

To speak divine mercy intelligibly, the myth itself must be reformed. The first most obvious requirement is that the myth be demasculinized. There is no excuse any longer for liturgical assemblies to cast biblical royal language in masculine form. Of the available English words, *sovereign* has perhaps the most weight, the deepest resonance, to render the Hebrew *melek* and the Greek *basileus*, usually translated "king." With some effort and artistry, the royal psalms can present a gender-neutral image of the sovereign, at least denying the assumption that the mighty one on top must be male. The word *sovereign* has the added advantage of connecting with contemporary political theories: British Christians call the queen their sovereign, and American Christians speak of sovereignty residing in the populace. The word, while not commonplace, is not archaic.

Not every occurrence of *king* in the Bible should be translated "sovereign," however. The ancient Hebrews wanted a king; Herod was a king: these uses of *king* heighten the contrast between our meager

---

19. James Davies, cited in R. W. Franklin, "Pusey and Worship in Industrial Society," *Worship* 57 (1983): 403–4.

earthly attempts at security and the religious image of divine sovereignty. When the biblical text refers generically to tribal leaders, *kings* may not be as felicitous or accurate as *monarchs* or *rulers*. Although they did not get very good press, queens, after all, did exist in biblical Israel. A helpful translation technique would be reliance on verbs. That God is sovereign can be rendered "God reigns."[20] Sometimes verbs can carry a force that nouns cannot. The Christian prayer is not that God fills the category of sovereign, but that God enacts justice and ensures stability. Verbs perhaps better than nouns can convey this religious idea by focusing on God's saving actions rather than on divine description.

The biblical phrase usually translated "the kingdom of God" must also be rendered in a gender-neutral way. That a monarchy remains a kingdom when its sovereign is a female demonstrates an androcentric linguistic prejudice that the head of state is male. *Queendom* is not a word. Use of the word *kingdom* renders God masculine even if king is carefully eliminated for God. Many aspects of the myth of the crown must be held together in creative tension for the biblical image of God's sovereignty to be fully articulated.[21] The biblical phrase imagines sometimes an earthly land on which God's people live; a heavenly time and space of spiritual abode; an interior divine direction within the faithful believer; and a perfected social order toward which the church slowly moves the world. An effective translation would offer space for all these biblical ideas to resonate.

Several options are available. The newly popular *reign of God* has as its greatest drawback that *reign* is a homonym of *rain*, an unfortunate infelicity considering that liturgical speech is primarily oral and aural, not written. *Rule of God* is too law-oriented. *Realm of God* is a possibility. *Dominion of God* has the advantage of connoting both a land mass and a spiritual state. At least in Canada, however, the word *dominion* came to signify foreign rule, and Canadians generally judge the word as

20. This technique is repeatedly used in the psalter project of the Roman Catholic International Commission on English in the Liturgy (ICEL). See Mary Collins, "Glorious Praise: The ICEL Liturgical Psalter," *Worship* 66 (1992): 290–310.

21. Wendell Willis, ed., *The Kingdom of God in 20th Century Interpretation* (Peabody, Mass.: Hendrickson, 1987), and Bruce Chilton, ed., *The Kingdom of God* (Philadelphia: Fortress, 1984), provide excellent summaries of the scholarly discussions.

inappropriate for an autonomous nation. *Commonwealth*, although seldom used in this context, deserves serious consideration. Its connotation of egalitarian well-being, of the parts working smoothly for the good of the whole, expresses much of the biblical hope for life within the beneficence of God.[22] It is interesting that the New Zealand/Maori Anglican liturgy provides a paraphrase of the Prayer of Jesus which casts "your kingdom come" as "Your commonwealth of peace and freedom sustain our hope and come on earth."[23] In general, however, the translation of *basileia* in the Prayer of Jesus will remain an enormous problem. That so many Christians resist bringing the language of particularly this prayer from the sixteenth century to the twentieth suggests that its use of *kingdom* will continue to reign for a long time to come.[24]

Decisions about how to render the language of Christ as king will depend on the context. In the narratives of the passion, the word *king* might be completely appropriate. Indeed, the liturgical wisdom to read John 18–19 on Good Friday, thus proclaiming the triumphant monarch on the day of the crucifixion, exemplifies the church's necessarily paradoxical use of the myth of the crown. In the doxological language of prayer and hymnody, however, language that raises Christ above male monarchs would be more felicitous. One recalls the problematic example of the myth of the crown in the classic eucharistic hymn "Gloria in Excelsis Deo." Translation of Scriptures and rendering of classic liturgical texts always require meticulous application of complex principles: one cannot simply program a computer to change all problematic language automatically. In every sentence one must judge whether the word choice conveys the most profound religious meaning sought by the context.

A beneficial liturgical restoration in recent times is baptismal anointing. The gospel democratizes the myth of the crown. Who is now reigning within the dominion of God? Who is anointed to be the heir of divine majesty? Not the male on top, but every single baptized

22. C. H. Dodd, *The Meaning of Paul for Today* (Cleveland: Meridian, 1957), 139–46.

23. *A New Zealand Prayer Book* (Auckland, New Zealand: Collins, 1989), 181.

24. The 1992 revision by the English Language Liturgical Consultation (ELLC) of the ordinary of the liturgy retains both occurrences of *kingdom* in the Prayer of Jesus.

person claims royal prerogatives. If the church is to continue to use the myth of the crown in relation to God and God's messiah, use of this myth should intensify as the gospel applies it to the dominion of God. Not only renewed use of the anointing, but also language highlighting baptism as coronation is appropriate.

Even were these benign translations and reforms to become the norm, the church must beware of expecting more from the myth of the crown than it can deliver. The Magnificat suggests that the incarnation sabotages the monarchy. Christianity turns the myth on its head: the son dies, and sovereignty is dispersed equally among all the citizens of the realm. Belief in the incarnation suggests at least these liturgical reforms: Absolutely no pictures or statues of God as a crowned and bearded monarch will appear in worship spaces, church buildings, or (especially) in children's catechetical material. Crosses will best not represent Christ as a robed and crowned figure. The point is not that Christ is a king who was crucified in a golden robe and a bejeweled diadem, but rather that kingship itself was crucified. It is doubtful whether this explicitly Christian idea is conveyed by the image of a crowned king on a cross. The Sunday commonly called the Reign of Christ could find its importance minimized. This liturgical glorification of the single image of Christ's kingship is a peculiar innovation of the twentieth century. Even were the church to retain eschatological themes at the conclusion of ordinary time, images of Christ as the feast, the garden, or the city could at least alternate with the image of Christ as king.

Ascension is another festival that enthrones Christ as king. Perhaps the best advice for this problematic festival is its gradual suppression. Fortunately its falling on a Thursday already diminishes its significance in the Christian calendar. Surely the church's most hopelessly archaic celebration, the day proclaims both the ancient myth of the crown and an antiquated cosmology. Pastorally the day usually becomes a disastrous observance of the absence of Christ in the community. The church could hear again the counsel of Pope Leo, that Ascension Day teaches that the presence of Christ has passed into the sacraments.[25] To remain religiously helpful, Ascension Day must somehow be recast. Were the church to judge the Lucan chronology of the resurrection appearances

---

25. Leo, "Sermon LXXIV," in *Nicene and Post-Nicene Fathers*, 2d series (New York: Christian Literature Company, 1895), 12:188.

important to enact, perhaps focusing on the number forty as a symbol of God's continuing presence with the people might salvage the day to proclaim not an ancient worldview, but divine mercy today.

The church's use of the myth of the crown must submit ever more attentively to the specific Christian message. The myth connects Christians with religious history and forms the foundation of Trinity language. But the myth always stands corrected by the incarnation. When the church uses the myth to revel in a reactionary past or to sanctify hierarchy or patriarchy in its own institution, the social order, or the human imagination, the myth becomes a diabolical tool that distorts the gospel. Of the myth of the crown, the Christian must finally say, as God said when harnessing the sea: only this far, and no farther.

seven

THE LANGUAGE OF TRINITARIAN DOCTRINE

Doctrine is a set of statements establishing the parameters for appropriate religious grammar. Because religious expression always borders on mystery, one statement is never sufficient to say the truth of the faith. In doctrinal formulations, each statement contributes one part of the whole, each correcting a tendency that other statements might suggest; for example, the implications of belief in one God are countered by belief in the Trinity. Thus to be Christian, one must say A, one must say also B, one may say M, R is extremely problematic, one cannot say Z. That many pairs of doctrinal statements are paradoxical allows for considerable latitude in Christian speech; that doctrine functions as outside limits keeps the church's prayer distinctively Christian. Every generation engages in the difficult task of keeping Christian language both animated by the paradoxes and guided by the limits.

The deceptively simple designation of God as Father, Son, and Spirit is an abbreviation of the extremely complex doctrine of the Trinity. This doctrine brilliantly systematized scriptural references about God's work of salvation, provided a philosophical framework for religious piety, and countered a progression of heresies, any one of which, had it become ascendant, would have effected a different Christianity, and some of which recur repeatedly in history. Many twentieth-century theologians believe that trinitarian language remains a portal, perhaps the only portal, to God. Nearly every serious contemporary theologian has tackled the Trinity, each offering a different corrective to the church's usually shallow, sometimes ludicrous, increasingly apologetic presentation of trinitarian doctrine.[1] Some theologians believe that Father,

---

1. See William J. Hill, O.P., *The Three-Personed God: The Trinity as the Mystery*

and Spirit is God's proper name, and as such its appropriateness cannot be questioned.[2] Some systematicians are able to dismiss quickly the questions and concerns of contemporary feminists in their defense of classic trinitarian doctrine.[3]

The intricate trinitarian discussions of the church's formative centuries, however, were not only intellectually stunning but also thoroughly androcentric. Some scholars argue that a radically different Christianity would have or could have been in some ways better than the one we inherited,[4] and some Christians seek to discard trinitarian language as arcane patriarchal philosophy. Both with and without the cooperation of the faithful, the trinitarian language of many praying communities is being pared down, if not edited out altogether. To remain an orthodox Christian, however, one can neither parrot the past nor jettison the Trinity: conservatives are too likely to do the first, liberals the second. Those who craft the liturgical prayers of the faithful must investigate both the ways in which doctrinal language of the Trinity is a portal to God—its paradoxes opening a way forward, its limits clarifying the gospel—and in what ways such trinitarian language obstructs reception of divine mercy.

Even defenders of trinitarian language would have to concur that *Father, Son, and Spirit* has to a considerable degree failed to convey the intended trinitarian meaning. There is plenty of fault to go around.

---

of Salvation (Washington, D.C.: Catholic University of America Press, 1982), 81–237, for a discussion of the trinitarian views of two dozen contemporary male theologians. See Elizabeth A. Johnson, *She Who Is: The Mystery of God in Feminist Theological Discourse* (New York: Crossroad, 1992), 205–11, and Ted Peters, *God as Trinity: Relationality and Temporality in Divine Life* (Louisville: Westminster/John Knox Press, 1993), for discussions of many current theologians' trinitarian proposals.

2. See, for example, Alvin Kimel Jr., "The God Who Likes His Name: Holy Trinity, Feminism, and the Language of Faith," in *Speaking the Christian God: The Holy Trinity and the Challenge of Feminism*, ed. Alvin Kimel Jr. (Grand Rapids: Eerdmans, 1992). Also Carl E. Braaten, "The Problem of God-Language Today," in *Our Naming of God: Problems and Prospects of God-Talk Today*, ed. Carl E. Braaten (Minneapolis: Fortress, 1989), 33. As a student of Robert Jenson in the 1970s, I argued this same position in "Lutheran Liturgical Prayer and God as Mother," *Worship* 52 (1978): 522.

3. Peters, *God as Trinity*, dismisses the charge of sexism in trinitarian language in several paragraphs, 53–55.

4. See Elisabeth Schüssler Fiorenza, *In Memory of Her: A Feminist Theological Reconstruction of Christian Origins* (New York: Crossroad, 1984).

The philosophical ideas underlying the speech are complex; and essential links, such as the incorporation of the Greek Logos idea into ancient son-language, are often omitted. Some theologians used father-language for other than trinitarian purposes: Martin Luther, for example, wrote that God the Father is the model of all father figures who require obedience.[5] Systematicians write obfuscations and then ridicule the faithful for their inability to understand. Popular catechesis has misconstrued trinitarian language and consequently mistaught it. Twentieth-century psychology has trained modern ears to hear language of father-and-son in ways never dreamed of by the Cappadocians. For example, the father-and-son language used in teaching the substitutionary theory of atonement sounds to contemporary hearers like a narrative of child abuse.[6] Western art, by repeatedly setting before the worshiping assembly a depiction of an old man, a young man, and a third thing, has seared into Christian imagination the twofold misconception that *Father* implies that God is an old man and that *three persons* implies that God is three separate beings.[7]

THE WORD *FATHER*

Christian meaning of the word *Father* originated long before Christian beginnings. We have already noted that in the Hebrew tradition, father-language is a consequence of the myth of the crown. The king is the son of God. By a logic inherent in a patriarchal culture, God is consequently the father of the king, and if of the crown, then by extension of the people. Father-language is rare in the Hebrew Scriptures.[8] When it occurs, it is metaphoric imagery describing the unique relationship

5. Martin Luther, "Large Catechism," in *The Book of Concord*, ed. Theodore G. Tappert (Philadelphia: Fortress, 1959), 379–89.

6. See, for example, the seventeenth-century hymn by Paul Gerhardt, "A Lamb Goes Uncomplaining Forth," in *Lutheran Book of Worship* (Minneapolis: Augsburg Publishing House, 1978), #118.

7. In the church I attended as a child, the massive chancel mural depicted the Father as a bearded old man, the Son as a long-haired young man bare to the waist, and the Spirit as an ermine-cloaked and hooded figure with a shining hand upraised. Someone once suggested to me that my entire scholarly career is in reaction to that mural: perhaps so. Mercifully, the church building no longer stands.

8. Gail Ramshaw Schmidt, "Lutheran Liturgical Prayer and God as Mother," 525–26.

between the chosen people and their deity, who is increasingly under-stood as the single god of the universe. The language in the Hebrew Scriptures is not intended literally: that is, ancient Jewish stories do not suggest that YHWH actually procreated to produce the king or the people. Furthermore, the idea that the God of the chosen people is father of the whole universe or of all the world's people is alien to the Hebrew tradition. Rather, because the king of Israel is the son of God, God can be imagined as father of the faithful.

The first-century Jews surrounding Jesus, however, were not living in an exclusively Hebrew culture. Under Caesar Augustus's patriarchal order, *Pater patriae*, father of the fatherland, was adopted as the title of the emperor, and pious Jews called YHWH "father" in protest.[9] In some Greco-Roman texts, *Father* functioned as a synonym for God.[10] According to Greco-Roman legends, Zeus, then Jupiter, was literally the father of the many beings he had procreated through actual sexual intercourse. One example of the Greco-Roman Zeus-Jupiter appeared in Hebrew culture when the Septuagint cast El Shaddai as *Pantokrator*; here the Greek idea of the omnipotent deity was substituted for the more explicitly Hebrew revelation of God. The late Wisdom literature of the Hellenized Jews evidenced a rigid patriarchalism rooted not within the Hebrew nomadic tradition, but within the Greek city-state. The search for the trinitarian meaning of *Father* is conducted in the crowded field of Greco-Roman religious, political, social, and linguistic fathers.

Thus while there is no doubt that during the first century Christians popularized the language of *Father*,[11] the origin of such speech remains elusive. The theory proposed by Joachim Jeremias and permeating the Christology of mid-century, that Jesus' unique experience of God as Abba was the root of Christianity,[12] is now judged insupportable.[13]

9. Mary Rose D'Angelo, "*Abba* and 'Father': Imperial Theology and the Jesus Tradition," *Journal of Biblical Literature* 111 (1992): 623–27.

10. Walter Burkert, *Greek Religion* (Cambridge, Mass.: Harvard University Press, 1985), 129–30.

11. Data are available in Ramshaw Schmidt, "Lutheran Liturgical Prayer and God as Mother," 526–28.

12. Joachim Jeremias, *The Prayers of Jesus* (Naperville, Ill.: Allenson, 1967), 29, 97, 111.

13. See Ruth C. Duck, *Gender and the Name of God: The Trinitarian Baptismal Formula* (New York: Pilgrim Press, 1990), 63–69, for one summary of objections.

Considerable debate has been put forth concerning to what degree calling God *Abba* in Aramaic, or its Hellenized version *Pater*, characterized the primitive Christian movement. One theory suggests that, far from an expression of intimacy, *Abba* invoked God as the one granting spiritual power to the suffering martyr.[14] We cannot at the present time determine whether Jesus or the early Christians saw *Abba* as a unique revealed divine name or, quite the contrary, whether Christians, using the Greek language of their culture, incorporated into their religion the stereotypical pagan title for the head of the pantheon.

A third root must be acknowledged here. In the ancient Western world, human procreation was inaccurately understood. Aristotle's theory asserted that the entire substance of the human infant resided in the father's sperm. The mother's womb passively received the sperm and provided some of the matter of the developing child.[15] If the mother received the sperm fully and well, a male child developed; if she received it less well, a female child developed. The notion that in the sperm was the whole essential human being, a male human being if perfectly received, was accepted in the West until the scientific revolution. Early medical drawings, for example, popularized this idea by depicting the sperm as a minute fetus.

It is staggering to imagine the effect of this erroneous biology on theological speculation. For example, to Luke the virgin birth meant not what many contemporary believers imagine, that Mary's egg was miraculously fertilized. Luke, not knowing about eggs, uses this language rather to affirm that Jesus came wholly from God. The fourth-century Cappadocian Fathers, whose linguistic formulations about the Trinity became Christian orthodoxy, asserted that *Father* means "the Unoriginate Origin," that is, the absolute origin of all.[16] Because medieval biology understood human identity as coming wholly from the father, father terminology flourished; supposedly scientifically accurate language was appropriated for complex descriptions of the divine. As the centuries progressed, the misogynist bias in celibate theological

14. Mary Rose D'Angelo, "Theology in Mark and Q: *Abba* and 'Father' in Context," *Harvard Theological Review* 85 (1992): 161.

15. Aristotle, *Generation of Animals*, Loeb Classical Library 13 (Cambridge. Mass.: Harvard University Press, 1979), 101–7.

16. Catherine Mowry LaCugna, *God for Us: The Trinity and Christian Life* (San Francisco: HarperCollins, 1991), 60–66.

circles intensified the linking of the father with life to the exclusion of the mother.

With these three roots identified—the several biblical uses of the term *Father*, the Greco-Roman cultural and linguistic system using *Father* synonymously with *God*, and an Aristotelian biology assuming the father as the origin—we come to the doctrinal flowering of trinitarian speech. Early theologians, in ordering biblical language about the God who saves, present the pre-Nicene consensus that God the Father creates, redeems, and divinizes through the Son in the Spirit.[17] Some theologians emphasized the three—God saved through Christ in the Spirit—and others the one—the first person working through the second and third persons. To avoid the subordination of the Son characteristic of the Arian heresy, the Cappadocians stated that Christ was "eternally begotten" (these two words in themselves creating an oxymoron) from the Unoriginated Origin. The prepositions *through* the Son and *in* the Spirit were replaced by *and*: the Father and the Son and the Holy Spirit are grammatically rendered equal.[18] This emphasis on "three persons," leaning toward tritheism, called for a counterbalance that never materialized.

While theologians have suggested many metaphoric images for God—for example, Tertullian's root, the tree, and the fruit, or fountain, the river, and the stream;[19] or Julian's maker, lover, and keeper[20]—those theologians who formulated trinitarian doctrine did not claim that father-son language is metaphor. The Cappadocians explicitly denied that calling the first person "the Father of the Son" suggests that God is like a father.[21] Early theologians speak as if Father, Son, and Spirit are labels rather than images, claiming that God comes with the biblical name Father, since the first person is the origin of the (eternally begotten) second, not that God acts like a father and thus acquires the title metaphorically. Christians can no longer accept classical theologians' assertions, however, without inquiring behind their disclaimers

17. Ibid., 23.

18. Ibid., 127.

19. Tertullian, "Against Praxeas," in *The Ante-Nicene Fathers*, ed. Alexander Roberts and James Donaldson (Grand Rapids: Eerdmans, 1963), 3:603.

20. Juliana of Norwich, *Revelations of Divine Love*, trans. M. L. Del Mastro (Garden City, N.Y.: Doubleday & Company, 1977), 87.

21. LaCugna, *God for Us*, 57.

to their unconscious reasons for canonizing *Father* as a divine name. The Bible itself uses *father* as a model for God, both as the father known in loving care (see the Sermon on the Mount, Matt. 6:25-33) and as the autocratic patriarch characterized by harsh discipline (see Heb. 12:5-11, although the New Revised Standard Version's use of *parent* disguises the original meaning). Many contemporary theologians, in contrast with the theologians of the fourth century, begin with the assumption that father-language is indeed a metaphoric model, which Christian kerygma must continually amend.[22]

Augustine anthropomorphized trinitarian language by writing that God is like the Lover, the Beloved, and Love[23] and that the Trinity is like human memory, understanding, and will.[24] Augustine's projection of the human psyche into God contributed substantially to the humanization of God, which evolved for fifteen hundred years into a masculinized Trinity. This cultural tendency was unchecked by serious theology. Medieval theologians were increasingly caught up in speculation, not about God's relation to humanity, but about the Trinity's being in itself.[25] This so-called immanent Trinity, perhaps a theological masterpiece, became a religious failure. Trinitarian theology abandoned its primary task, helping Christians pray, for another pursuit, philosophically describing divinity. Not in the Middle Ages, and not in the twentieth century, are the majority of Christians interested in the being of God within God. The faithful have sought to be connected to God, and the names of God recurring in the church's prayer life provide this primary connection. *Father* came to mean not Abba, not resistance to emperor worhip, not the philosophical Unoriginate Origin, not the key to Christology, but a personalized masculine authority figure. Zeus has won.

Many contemporary Christians find themselves, like Socrates, unmasking their religious language about the divine to expose a meager

---

22. See, for example, Ian T. Ramsey, *Religious Language: An Empirical Placing of Theological Phrases* (New York: Macmillan, 1957), 203–5, and Sallie McFague, *Models of God: Theology for an Ecological, Nuclear Age* (Philadelphia: Fortress, 1987), 33.

23. Augustine, "On the Holy Trinity," in *A Select Library of Nicene and Post-Nicene Fathers,* ed. Philip Schaff (Buffalo: Christian Literature Company, 1887), 3:204.

24. Ibid., 143.

25. LaCugna, *God for Us,* 167–68.

mythological father. If the word *Father* is neither literally nor meta-phorically defensible, and if it automatically introduces ideas alien to orthodox doctrine, its continued constant usage must be questioned. The fundamentalist assertion that *Father* is a biblically revealed name, neither a metaphor nor psychological projection, must give a more adequate answer to these queries, for the controversy is all around us. Some women claim alienation from the father image. Devout Christians are producing worship resources that minimize or wholly avoid father-language. Some current trinitarian prayers substitute *Mother* for *Father*. Divine mother-language, only recently anathema, is increasingly woven into hymns, prayers, and sermons in much of mainstream Christianity. [26] Such replacing *Father* with *Mother* reflects the current cultural bias that the mother is the dominant (if not indeed the sole) parent, a notion no more biologically accurate, sexually ethical, or religiously helpful than Aristotle's. The most serious result of diluting father imagery, however, is that it usually occasions the disappearance of the Trinity. To the extent that the Christian God was reduced to a father, the Trinity was already moribund. Christian prayer cannot ignore the extent to which the language of the Trinity is on life-support and *Father* an embarrassment, as well as the unlikelihood that *Mother* can meet current expectations.

THE CATEGORY *PERSON*

A second obstacle to orthodox trinitarian faith is the theological lan-guage of *person*. In the fourth century, theologians speaking Greek described God as one divine essence in three *hypostases*; those speaking Latin spoke of one divine substance in three *personae*. That *hypostasis* and *persona* came to be cast in English as *person* complicates considerably our reception of the trinitarian mystery. In most contexts, our culture uses the word *person* to mean a center of consciousness, an individual identity. The psychological movement, so influential in contemporary thought, focuses attention on the person and the person's personality as the unique essence of the human being. Many twentieth-century theologians agree that the term *person* must be replaced. Even Augustine remarked, "If we say three persons, it is not so much to affirm something

26. See chap. 8 for a discussion of mother-language.

as to avoid saying nothing."[27] Karl Barth suggested the phrase "modes of being," Karl Rahner "ways of being."[28] In contemporary American English, language of "three persons" strengthens the tritheism suggested by "the Father and the Son and the Holy Spirit." Although liberals tend to stress the unitarian nature of God, conservatives concur that the Trinity is essential for Christian truth. Yet no creative proposals which express that Trinity in contemporary categories are popularized, and the faithful are still taught the formula "three persons in one God" and sing it regularly in hymnody.

Because father-son language, despite the theologians' disclaimers, functions as an anthropomorphic model, *person* language compounds the problem by in yet another way implying the Trinty to be a committee of three persons. The nineteenth-century piety that focused on the man Jesus walking at the Christian's side contributed to the humanizing of the divine; however, calling Christ "the second person" offers no corrective to "the man Jesus," since *person* is heard as a synonym of *man*. The problem with *person* will intensify as the word is increasingly used to replace *man* as a gender-neutral designation for the human being.

Some theologians hope that appropriate use of *the divine person* can help define *the human person* better. Catherine LaCugna makes an impressive argument that *person* means not a center of consciousness but a being in relation, and that the ability to be in relation with others is the primary meaning of personhood.[29] Some feminists maintain that Western culture must transfer its values from an obsessive individualism typified in the isolated male person back to the reality of the common good, a value more fully realized by women in relation to one another.[30] One can see in many areas of our culture attempts to rediscover and retrieve the communal matrix of the individual person, but whether the word *person* can be energized to convey the Trinity seems unlikely.

27. Augustine, "On the Holy Trinity," 92, 109–10.
28. Hill, *The Three-Personed God*, 117, 144.
29. LaCugna, *God for Us*, 288–92.
30. See, for example, Elizabeth H. Fox-Genovese, *Feminist without Illusion: A Critique of Individualism* (Chapel Hill: University of North Carolina Press, 1991), 225–41.

THE GENIUS OF TRINITARIAN THEOLOGY

Despite its problematic terminology, trinitarian doctrine is Christianity's strongest defense against classical patriarchal monotheism.[31] The God worshiped by the church is not a masculine monarch, the outside authority residing beyond the skies. Rather, the Trinity is the model of interrelatedness, the image of order without subordination, the God both beyond and within, and it is this deity that Christian language must attempt to describe and praise.

If *person* implies a center of rationality, language of *three persons* misconstrues Christian intent. To the extent that a person is a being in relation, however, *three persons* models the interrelatedness of all that is. To be is to be in relation to others. Some feminist theory, for example in political science,[32] psychology,[33] and linguistics,[34] suggests that women (or many women), either by genetic determination or social development, are more attuned than men (or many men) to this interrelatedness of all humans and of humans to the wider creation. Not only feminists have considered human nature in terms of relationality rather than rationality. The psychiatrist Harry Stack Sullivan, for example, defined the person as what has emerged in a lifetime of relationships.[35] His theory doubted that emotional health could ever be secured in isolation. Since every person is the total of that person's relationships, healing comes about, Sullivan observed, through new and renewed relationships.

Trinitarian doctrine states that not even God is a monad, a being in isolation. God is in relation with the world. God created the world, loves it, and continuously inspires it to love. It is impossible to imagine the biblical God before creation, for the God as experienced by Israel

---

31. See, for example, Jürgen Moltmann, *History and the Triune God: Contributions to Trinitarian Theology* (New York: Crossroad, 1992), 20–22.

32. Fox-Genovese, *Feminism without Illusion*.

33. Carol Gilligan, *In a Different Voice: Psychological Theory and Women's Development* (Cambridge, Mass.: Harvard University Press, 1982), and Nancy Chadorow, *The Reproduction of Mothering: Psychoanalysis and the Sociology of Gender* (Berkeley: University of California Press, 1978).

34. Deborah Cameron, *Feminism and Linguistic Theory* (New York: St. Martin's Press, 1985).

35. Harry Stack Sullivan, *The Interpersonal Theory of Psychiatry* (New York: W. W. Norton, 1953), 18–20.

and the church is known always and only through divine relationship with the created world. Perhaps it is this understanding as God in relation that led to Jewish speculation about the realms of angels existing with God before the creation of the world: for God was always in relation. God's very being is relationship, which relationship the biblical language of Father, Son, and Spirit attempts to name. God's action in the world flows from an action within God. Thus the early theologians used the formula "the Father through the Son in the Spirit." Relatedness constitutes God.

A second assertion of trinitarian doctrine is that within God the relations are ordered without subordination. It is easy to imagine relatedness ordered in some pattern of subordination. The ancient myth of the crown is a picture of such subordination: the divine monarch is over the human monarch, who is over the people. Monarchical imagery of the one "at God's right hand" is an example of this stereotypical way to understand social order. So Arianism, strong in the fourth and twentieth centuries, understands Christ as a divine emissary, a half-human, half-divine figure subordinate to God the Father, and thus available to mediate human concerns. Orthodox trinitarian doctrine absolutely rejected this subordination and posited instead an order of coequals. Thus arose the paradoxical language that the Son was "eternally begotten": begotten, yes, but eternally: that is, there was never a time before the begottenness. The first person was not prior to the second, although the language of father-son implied it. Neither was the Spirit a vague divine power emanating from God, but a third person coequal in God.

One classical term used to articulate this coequality was *perichoresis*, the interdependence within God, a mutual yielding, the intermingling of God. Contemporary theologians are reviving this term,[36] seeing God's "divine dancing together"[37] as an image of love without subjection, order without subordination, care without mastery. Such *perichoresis* of the Trinity is an inspiration to feminists eager to find new patterns of living. History provides countless examples of the hierarchical ordering

36. See, for example, LaCugna, *God for Us*, 270–78, and Johnson, *She Who Is*, 220–21.

37. Patricia Wilson-Kastner, *Faith, Feminism, and the Christ* (Philadelphia: Fortress, 1983), 127.

of society. Legend says that Confucius brought order to China by commanding all the people to sit in their proper seats. But history affords few examples of productivity without subordination, of cooperation that does not naively deny difference. Persons are not identical in talent, experience, interest, responsibility. The Trinity's *perichoresis* suggests an image not of marching armies, with a man at the top ordering dispensable minions, but of dancing love, Dante's intermingling circles of light[38] that transform all who join in the dance.

A third assertion of trinitarian doctrine is that God is not dwelling beyond time and space, a divine being wholly disconnected from the world. Many eighteenth-century Americans who shaped American thought and life affirmed such a deist God, an Aristotelian First Cause no longer concerned about the creation set in motion eons ago. But the Trinity is a God known by our experiencing divine life for and in the world. The Trinity who is before time and beyond space is also born in this world, incarnate in Jesus Christ, living and dying as do human beings; and the Trinity is active in the human community, nurturing all good thought and action, keeping the world from disintegration into evil and chaos. Historically, the church debated whether God's Spirit is active also outside the church. Such a question now seems shortsighted. While the church can confidently testify to the Spirit's life within the body of Christ, the biblical record repeatedly proclaims a God surprisingly greater in creative mercy than the faithful can imagine. God's Spirit is not the universe itself, a universe shaped by cyclical life and death. Rather, God's merciful Spirit is the Living One who gives life to the entire world, procreating plants and animals, pouring out the seas and rivers, engendering human community, inspiring human love, promising life even beyond death.

That God is known as relatedness; that God is order without subordination; that God's divinity is not divorced from, but rather wed to, our humanity: these are astounding assertions about the Christian God all too often obscured in the church. Yet these joyous beliefs constitute Christianity, and if taught and celebrated, would construe Christianity to be the distinctive religion it hopes to be. The world already has enough patriarchal, or matriarchal, monotheism, and the

---

38. Dante Alighieri, *Paradise*, vol. 3, in *The Divine Comedy*, trans. Mark Musa (New York: Penguin Books, 1984), 393.

human race is too needy for deism. The Trinity—the God connected, the God intertwined, the God permeating—is the God of mercy for the church and the world.

THE TRINITY IN THE LITURGY

The church cannot continue to repeat classical Christian language, whether of father or of person, claim the words do not mean what people think they mean, and ignore the resulting confusion. If historic terminology is easily misunderstood, Christians must find alternate speech to assist the proclamation of divine mercy. Even Augustine acknowledged that trinitarian language was inadequate:

> The proper object of our enjoyment is the Father, Son, and Holy Spirit, a single Trinity, one supreme Being, accessible to all who enjoy it. . . . It is not easy to find a term which appropriately defines such great excellence, unless it is better to say that this Trinity is one God from whom, through whom and in whom all things exist.[39]

Here Augustine relies on alternate biblical language (Rom. 11:36) to elucidate the meaning of the Christian God. The Trinity is the one "from whom, through whom and in whom" all things exist, who is present before all, incarnate in history, the source of life today. Since *person* is comparatively rare in liturgical language, let us focus on *father*.

Those who claim Father as God's actual given name must answer much more convincingly than they have questions about the origin of this word in the Hebrew monarchy, in Greco-Roman culture, and its philosophical meaning during the early centuries of the church. Defense of Father, Son, and Spirit as the biblically mandated name of God is a fundamentalist argument, not particularly persuasive when it appears in support of one's pet ideas. If *father* is a technical theological term, rather like *hypostasis*, it has little place in the language of prayer. If *father* is a model, rather like *dove* or *fire*, then it must take its turn with other models that convey different aspects of divine truth.

Perhaps the way forward is via several parallel paths. The church must stop giving credence to theologians who in defending the Trinity make claims about God's name and sexual description that are far more

---

39. Augustine, "On Christian Doctrine," in *A Select Library of Nicene and Post-Nicene Fathers*, 2:524.

androcentric than the great theological tradition was. When the church uses Father, Son, and Spirit language, for example, in the ecumenical creeds, which are optional additions to the eucharistic liturgy, ways must be found to teach the meaning of this language. The language of father-son is meant to articulate Christology: the Father is Father of the Son, not primarily of the worshiper. No ultimate victory is to be found in destroying all positive content to the imagery of fatherhood, however. Father, Son, and Spirit language should be alternated with other models and formulations, each of which indicates some aspect of doctrinal truth, each of which needs correctives from other doctrinal formulations.[40] Augustine was correct that the language of Father, Son, and Spirit cannot fully embrace the mystery, and Christians gladly enrich their speech, for example, with the biblical phrase "from whom, through whom and in whom," to proclaim trinitarian faith.

Some of the most egregious misrepresentations of the Trinity are in liturgical art. In many churches murals, mosaics, banners, or bulletin covers hold up before the assembly a depiction of an old man, a young man, and perhaps a dove or a cloud. Such depictions find their way into church buildings despite the church's ancient wisdom concerning the inappropriateness of such art. As the Great Moscow Council declaimed in 1667, "To represent the God of Sabaoth (that is, the Father) on icons with a gray beard, with his only Son on his lap, and a dove between them, is exceedingly absurd and unseemly."[41] One step in reenlivening the Trinity is to rid Christian assemblies of such debased art, remaining ever vigilant lest such depictions pop up in children's catechesis, stunting the growth of their religious imagination.

Were images of the Trinity judged useful, the church could imitate the icon tradition in Eastern Orthodoxy that draws the three angels dining with Abraham and Sarah. In its most superb representation painted by Andrew Rublev, the *perichoresis* of the Trinity draws the viewer into the circle of holiness around the chalice.[42] The story of Noah's flood suggests the threefold depiction of the rainbow, the ark,

40. Even LaCugna, in her steadfast defense of the Trinity, usually writes "God" rather than "the Father." See *God for Us*, p. 18, n. 7.

41. Leonid Ouspensky and Vladimir Lossky, *The Meaning of Icons*, trans. G. E. nd E. Kadlowbovsky (Crestwood, N.Y.: St. Vladimir's Seminary Press,

198, 201–4.

and the dove: God creates the life of the universe, carries humanity through death, and effects a community of peace. The Christian tradition includes many illuminating metaphors to inspire artists: the Trinity as root, stem, and fruit; source, river, and stream; Catherine of Siena's table, food, and waiter;[43] and Dante's vision in Paradise of three interpenetrating circles of light. Drawing God, however, is probably not catechetically useful. The dominant Christian idea is that to see the Trinity, the church looks at the face of Christ and recognizes the Spirit within the Christian community. Perhaps the church should get completely out of the business of making graven images of the divine.

In some service orders, worship begins "in the name of the Father, and of the Son, and of the Holy Spirit," and the liturgy concludes with a benediction repeating this line. The repetition of "and of . . . and of" contributes to the potential tritheism of the line. The phrase "In the name of God, Father, Son, and Holy Spirit" is more suggestive of the one trinitarian God. As well, other biblical phrases may be substituted. The Pauline invocation "The grace of the Lord Jesus Christ, the love of God, and the communion of the Holy Spirit be with all of you" (2 Cor. 13:13) richly proclaims trinitarian mercy. The Aaronic benediction (Num. 6:24-26) can be interpreted by Christians as a splendid trinitarian blessing. The first phrase recalls God's blessing on all that is. How are Christians "kept," but in Christ: thus the second phrase praises the incarnation of God in the face of Christ, who personifies divine grace. The third phrase calls down the divine peace of the Spirit of the Living One. Because it is so rich in imagery, this benediction is more liturgically useful than the doctrinal formula of the standard Christian benediction.

Many Christians articulate trinitarian faith through the words of their hymns. It is important to distinguish between those hymns that open up trinitarian mystery from those that trivialize the faith. Both innovative and traditional hymns require attentive scrutiny. Alas, liturgical reformers alive in the 1960s find it hard to forget the line in "Sons of God": "So we'll meet the Trinity, And live with them forever."[44]

---

43. *The Prayers of Catherine of Siena*, ed. Suzanne Noffke, O.P. (New York: Paulist, 1983), 102.

44. James Thiem, "Sons of God," in *Hymnal for Young Christians* (Chicago: F.E.L. Publications, 1966), 98–99. It is possible that the "them" refers back, ungrammatically, to "all men" in a previous line.

The past offers some treasures, however. St. Patrick's Breastplate presents archaic yet dynamic images of the Trinity.[45] Interestingly, the popular "Holy, Holy, Holy" by Reginald Heber, inspired by the songs and sets of the Book of Revelation, does not use Father, Son, and Spirit language, but by the threefold repetition of "Holy" and the phrase "God in three persons" acclaims the Trinity.[46] In some hymns, many images are interwoven. For example, John Marriott's hymn on the Trinity refers to word, light, healing, spirit, truth, dove, and lamp, and calls the Trinity "wisdom, love, might."[47] Sylvia Dustan's fine hymn "O Mystery Profound" calls God breather, breathing, breath.[48] How anthropomorphisms are handled is worth checking. Jeffrey Rowthorn's "Creating God" grants God fingers, hands, arms, and a face, without using the male models of father and son.[49] An increasing number of published hymns edit older texts or present creative language for trinitarian praise, although some texts have not yet matured beyond didactic rebuttals of traditional imagery.[50]

Currently the most controverted issue involving trinitarian language is the text of baptism. Echoing medieval debates over sacramental validity, one now hears quarrels about whether baptism "in the name of Jesus" constitutes valid baptism, despite the fact that as far into the Christian tradition as Thomas Aquinas theologians granted that baptism into the name of Jesus was exactly the same as baptism into the Triune name.[51] The church needs first to acknowledge that the traditional baptismal formula is not above misunderstanding. Ruth Duck, after carefully examining the theological advantages and disadvantages of several current adaptations of the traditional formula, demonstrates that

45. See, for example, its translation by James Quinn as "This Day God Gives Me," in *Worship III* (Chicago: GIA Publications, 1986), #673.

46. Reginald Heber, "Holy, Holy, Holy," in *Lutheran Book of Worship*, #165.

47. John Marriott, "God, Whose Almighty Word," in *Lutheran Book of Worship*, #400.

48. Sylvia Dunstan, "O Mystery Profound," in *In Search of Hope and Grace. 40 Hymns and Gospel Songs* (Chicago: GIA Publications, 1991), 23.

49. Jeffrey Rowthorn, "Creating God," in *The United Methodist Hymnal* (Nashville: United Methodist Publishing House, 1989), #109.

50. *The United Methodist Hymnal* exhibits some adroit editing and substitutions in classsic hymnody; for example, see Charles Wesley's "Maker, In Whom We Live," *The United Methodist Hymnal*, #88.

51. Thomas Aquinas, *Summa Theologiae*, 3a.66.6.

the phrase "baptism into the name of Father, Son, and Spirit" referred actually to the threefold questions at baptism, and she suggests adapting these questions without use of androcentric categories.[52] As a helpful exercise theologians might take up the challenge of constructing an orthodox baptismal text for a language that does not have words for father and son. The question remains: How can the mystery best be conveyed? One solution is, recalling Augustine, to baptize "in the name of the Triune God, from whom, through whom, and in whom all things exist, now and forever."

In the Sunday liturgy the eucharistic prayer most fully expresses trinitarian doctrine. In this long prayer the Christian assembly stands in thanksgiving before the Triune God, praising God for the world's creation and for its continued existence. With at least the presider's arms upraised in gratitude, worshipers recall God's gifts of life in the flowering of the universe and in the unfolding of human history. They praise God's connection to the millions of galaxies, to the configuration within the atom, and to the centuries of struggling human beings. They believe God to be not only the origin of all, but the perpetual nurturer and protector of all.

Since it is Christians who offer this thanksgiving, the prayer recognizes that this creation of the world climaxed in the incarnation. God is intertwined with humankind by having lived and died as one of the lowly of the world. God's human life, quite other than patriarchy might suggest, was lived not as a king, a man of great power and the father of many sons, but as a nobody, dismissed by the religious and executed by the authorities. The eucharistic prayer affirms that this intertwining of God with the human race mercifully continues in the meal here celebrated.

The prayer concludes by invoking this God to be in and among the community and the whole earth. This Spirit of the Triune God permeates the meal, rendering bread and wine the body of the divine; enlivens the assembly, forming the baptized into the body of the divine; and, worshipers pray, will at the end of time re-create the entire universe. The Spirit of God will turn the world, not into God, but to God, of which the transformation at this meal is a sign.

52. Duck, *Gender and the Name of God*, 185–87.

That the eucharistic prayer is trinitarian does not mean that it repeats the words *Father, Son,* and *Spirit.* The classic terminology might contribute toward or might detract from the prayer's being profoundly trinitarian. The prayer should be trinitarian in its deepest sense, in its conception and reception of God. The eucharistic prayer inserts the faithful into the trinitarian God, the God connected, intertwined, and permeating all that is, the God from whom, through whom, and in whom all things exist. Trinitarian language will survive, and help Christians survive, not if it remains merely doctrinal discourse, but only if its doctrine illumines the paradoxes and presents the limits by opening Christians to God's very self and God's very self to Christians. To that end, the church must continually search for better, truer, clearer, more faithful language about the God it knows as triune.

eight

ANTHROPOMORPHIC METAPHORS FOR GOD

To think about anthropomorphisms for God, one begins by listening to the ancient Hebrew people and discovering a mixed message. The Torah makes clear that metaphoric depiction of the divine is forbidden: no graven images. Yet although Judaism obeyed the letter of this law by rejecting humanlike statues to represent God, Hebrew poetry is replete with human metaphors for the divine. God is praised as warrior and judge, shepherd and potter, husband and mother. What the sculptors were denied, the poets celebrated. Thus the biblical record is a clear model for human conduct; the theological assertion that God is wholly other meets the human hope that a likeness exists between Creator and creature. Often the human hope wins the day.

METAPHOR ALONE

Contemporary linguistic theorist Paul Ricoeur taught that human language is nothing other than metaphoric speech within a community of discourse.[1] That is, words in a language have no distinct meaning apart from the sentence or outside the context. A word has meaning only by application of a previous connection to a new situation. Most words have several meanings, and words are always open to more meanings by application to new contexts. All human speech is characterized by the transfer of meaning from previous context to new context, from smaller matrix to larger, from one connotation to another. In its sharpest form, this transfer of meaning is called metaphor. "The

1. Paul Ricoeur, *The Rule of Metaphor*, trans. Robert Czerny (Toronto: University of Toronto Press, 1977), 101–33.

power of metaphor would be to break an old categorization, in order to establish new logical frontiers on the ruins of their forerunners,"[2] writes Ricoeur (metaphorically, of course).

If Ricoeur is correct that all human speech is metaphoric, religious language is preeminently metaphoric. To imagine the divine is by necessity to reach beyond human categories. Thus words about the divine must always be nuanced, modified, even negated by thinking worshipers. Theology chides the believer into seeing the inadequacy of religious speech. Meanwhile, the religious community establishes the context in which the appropriate meaning is perceived and received. The assembly of believers, the community of discourse, clarifies what the self-contradictory language means and how such meaning functions.

A community wishes to speak of or to God, or a visionary experiences divine mercy. Although the arts and nonverbal gesture assist in communicating religious experience, words are required if human speech to God and to one another of God is to be specific and clear. The visionary and the assembly transfer words from another context to the new context, hoping that the situation will make clear which of the old connotations are abandoned, which retained, and which transformed. This pattern of adapting preexisting words, what poets call metaphor, is not an optional practice that the church might try to do without. Although John Calvin's disciples rigorously whitewashed over the images painted on their churches' interior walls, their assemblies fiercely enforced the singing of the metaphor-laden psalter. Similarly, the mystics who taught the *via negativa* prayed the daily office and attended the Eucharist regularly: their acknowledgment of the limits of religious language and their adoption of contemplative silence coexisted with their continuous participation in a highly metaphoric liturgy.

An earlier ontology conceived of metaphor as dispensable. Christians confront this idea in Thomas Aquinas when he posits a distinction between analogy and metaphor.[3] Aquinas knew that metaphor is balanced on inaccuracy, and he wanted more surety in his speech about God. Against a Neoplatonic conception of being in the universe, with its chain of continuity between all that exists, such Aristotelian accuracy

---

2. Ibid., 197.
3. Thomas Aquinas, *Summa Theologiae*, 1a.13.5.

was possible by the Thomistic claim that analogy was unique religious language which was defined not by extension of human thought, but top-down, by revelation of the divine life. As God's self-revelation, analogy articulated accurately something of God's actual being to humankind. Aquinas believed analogy to be trustworthy because it was based on and expressed the connection between the being of the Creator and that of the creature. Thus for Aquinas *the One Who Is* is the best name for God, because it conveys solely the mystery of *esse*, the being which is God alone.[4]

Within a Thomistic understanding of analogy, the truth of the similarity between God and the human being is the starting position. The human tendency to create God in our own image, however, must contend with the dissimilarity between Creator and creature and with the inaccuracy of human categories. As the famous dictum from the Fourth Lateran Council said it, "However great the similarity between Creator and creature may be, the dissimilarity always nevertheless remains greater."[5] Aquinas taught that metaphors must be handled with extreme care, because metaphors move further and further from pure analogy by entertaining too much dissimilarity. Because traditional theology was leery of metaphor, anthropomorphisms for God were limited. The few approved anthropomorphisms then constituted a powerful graven image; yet sophisticated theology could deny that the metaphor was truly or profoundly Christian. We have already seen how this system entrenched the myth of the crown and the anthropomorphism of the king, and yet by disparaging metaphor theologians could wash their hands of the actual functioning of the metaphoric language in the imagination of the faithful.

For some Christians, Thomism remains a foundation for theological speculation.[6] For others, it is more like a medieval city wall, partly broken down and no longer militarily useful, but an important historic legacy that still dominates the landscape. The current defense of certain

---

4. Ibid., 1a.13.11.

5. Heinrich Denzinger, *The Sources of Catholic Dogma*, trans. Roy J. Deferrari (St. Louis: Herder, 1957), 171.

6. See, for example, William J. Hill, O.P., *The Three-Personed God: The Trinity as the Mystery of Salvation* (Washington, D.C.: Catholic University of America Press, 1982), 255–58, and Elizabeth A. Johnson, *She Who Is: The Mystery of God in Feminist Theological Discourse* (New York: Crossroad, 1992), 236–40.

language as the biblically revealed name of God recalls Thomistic arguments by positing certain formulations as more trustworthy than mere metaphor. For other twentieth-century Christians, Thomistic analogy is rejected as resting on an outmoded ontology. Not surprisingly, it is some of the theologians of the Reformation tradition,[7] with its sense of the great gulf fixed between the divine and the human and with its philosophical roots in nominalism, who have retired the theory of analogy and who see the church as speaking only in the ambivalence of metaphor.

The search for surety in religious language continues. Currently some theologians are marking the classic distinction between more and less trustworthy speech by using the categories *metaphor* and *simile*. Citing nineteenth-century grammatical definitions, Roland Frye distinguishes biblical metaphor, which speaks more accurate truth, for example, God as father, from simile, which utilizes less appropriate speech, for example, God as mother.[8] This argument, which uses the word *metaphor* differently than Thomism did, nonetheless demonstrates the identical tendency of theologians to protect the categories essential to their system with divine sanction and to distance the core of the faith from language they find problematic. Despite this understandable tendency, the twentieth-century church cannot claim some words as God-given labels that convey divine truth unambiguously. All the church has is what this book calls metaphor within a community of discourse,[9] the community here being the church. Human imagination offers the metaphors; theologians prod and shape, correct and deny the metaphors; the worshiping assembly, formed by the Spirit of Christ, informed by both its imagination and the correctives, says "yes" to the nuanced meaning of the metaphor. Yes, no, yes.

7. Wolfhart Pannenberg, *Basic Questions in Theology*, trans. George H. Kehm (Philadelphia: Fortress, 1970), 1:211–38.

8. Roland M. Frye, "Language for God and Feminine Language: Problems and Principles," in *Speaking the Christian God: The Holy Trinity and the Challenge of Feminism*, ed. Alvin Kimel Jr. (Grand Rapids: Eerdmans, 1992), 36–42. In the same collection also see Elizabeth Achtemeier, "Exchanging God for 'No Gods': A Discussion of Female Language for God," 4.

9. See Sallie McFague, *Models of God: Theology for an Ecological, Nuclear Age* (Philadelphia: Fortress, 1987), 31–40.

METAPHOR IN CHRISTIAN SPEECH

Christian religious language offers surprising answers to the world's perennial questions. Is life a chaotic spin into oblivion? No, the origin, the focus, and the goal of life is God. Is the deity exacting, distant, and arbitrary? No, God is merciful, incarnate, and present, revealed and reliable. Is this deity the male tip of a pyramid built on human shoulders? No, God is an interaction of love undergirding human freedom. That there is a God and that God is merciful: these are the fundamental surprises that Christian language seeks to convey, and for such surprising proposals metaphor is required. Whether in contemporary poetry or liturgical language, metaphor is the vehicle for repositioning old boundaries and for proposing new insight.

The surprises proliferate. If you thought that life is a precarious struggle for survival and safety, the faith tells you that God is your shepherd. If you experience life as perpetual injustice, the righteous suffering under the dominant wicked, the faith tells you that God is judge. If you fear that enemies will destroy your very life, the faith tells you that God is a warrior commanding your troops. If you feel that even your religious community has been abandoned by God, you are reminded that God is a nursing mother who cannot forget the chosen people.

The surprise is double. If you thought at first that life was a dread existence and any deity an alien power, you hear instead of overflowing mercy from one who can be likened to human beings. But there is a surprise underneath the surprise. The anthropomorphisms—God as shepherd, judge, warrior, mother—are only metaphors. However humans in such roles would fail, God will not. In any way that these anthropomorphisms are limited, God is not. The anthropomorphic metaphors have surprised us with mercy, but we come to know that even our most profound metaphors must be surprised by what is God. The metaphors counter our terror: each metaphor counters the other metaphors; but finally, all metaphors are countered by God.

In an ancient story found in Exodus 33, Moses intercedes before God. Moses has pleaded with God for a more definitive divine presence among the pilgrim people. How can the traveling Hebrew tribes trust confidently in God, unless God's presence and power are more visible and apparent? "Show me your glory, I pray," demands Moses. Here the story turns to anthropomorphism. By hiding in the cleft of the rock,

Moses can see the divine backside. God's face is too much to see, but God's back is full of mercy, and God's hand shields Moses from more divine presence than he could bear.

This amazing story illustrates faith's double surprise. Yes, there is a God, a powerful God, a merciful God, who can be imagined anthropomorphically. But God's presence is far more than God's back or hand or face: these are metaphoric concessions God makes to meet Moses' need. The narrative suggests that God's back is enough to fill human need, but that God is far more than such an anthropomorphism could convey, that God is much greater than a humanlike face could contain.

This pattern becomes normative in Christianity. According to the Christian Scriptures, one sees divine mercy most clearly by looking at Christ. "Show us the Father, and we will be satisfied," says a disciple in John 14; "Whoever has seen me has seen the Father," replies Jesus. Early Christians maintained the Jewish proscription against drawing images of God, but they began to draw the figure of Jesus as a kind of divine backside. In the incarnation are layers of metaphor: in his ministry Jesus acts metaphorically, bringing life into the world in healing miracles, teaching divine mercy by means of bewildering parables. Orthodox theology came to acknowledge Christ as more than a divine metaphor, as the actual face of God. The incarnation of God in Christ gave Christianity license to explore metaphors of a deity who suffers, bleeds, bears, and feeds. Christ has conquered evil; and so Christ, who is God for humanity, is a soldier. Christ suffers and bleeds to bear the believers; thus in the categories of a fourteenth-century woman, Christ, who is God for humanity, is her mother. [10]

Because faith believes that God is embodied in Christ, Christianity is especially open to the dangers of religious anthropomorphism. Christians can too easily believe the metaphors of God that arise in praise of Christ. The pervasiveness of pictures of Jesus as the good shepherd has undoubtedly suggested to many that Jesus not only made his living as a shepherd, but (especially in the minds of those for whom pictures demonstrate facts) is in some literal way humanity's shepherd. That the Bible in the first place transfers the shepherd image from describing

10. Juliana of Norwich, *Revelations of Divine Love*, trans. M. L. Del Mastro (Garden City, N.Y.: Doubleday, 1977), 190–92.

the king to describing God; that in Near Eastern cultures, ancient and modern, young women as well as young men worked as shepherds; and that the Christian Scriptures are employing metaphor when applying this image to Jesus: these nuances tend to get obscured by the Sunday school art.

When a metaphor no longer surprises, the literary critic calls it a dead metaphor. Too many metaphors in Christian speech are dead, dead, dead. They may be dead because the world of thought from which they are transferred is alien. For example, the current effort to retrieve the Sophia image must first reconstruct the world of the sages and wisdom goddesses: not an easy task. When catechesis employs only a few metaphors, some get worked to death. Christians come to expect Jesus to be described as a king and are no longer struck by the incongruity of such a religious claim. Other metaphors are killed because, especially to a literal-minded generation, they come to be believed. For example, if Jesus is understood to be literally a judge, solely at the moment of death, the metaphor of God as judge has been factualized and has lost its metaphoric power. All too often the church uses metaphor to conclude the religious quest rather than to spur it on in wonder.

The final danger inherent in the practice of anthropomorphism is atheism. If the metaphor stops at Jesus, if Jesus is the Christian's friend or mother or judge or shepherd, the result can be a Jesus-centered religion in which a man who lived a long time ago becomes an icon of religious security. Just as, depending on the century, the metaphor of judge or friend can become all there is to Christ, so the image of Jesus can become all there is of God. When Christianity becomes a fantasy about a man, it indeed cannot save a woman, or a man either. The anthropomorphisms must continue to surprise, dropping the believer finally in amazement in the lap of God.

METAPHORS FROM HUMAN OCCUPATIONS

The Scriptures often ascribe to God human occupations: God is judge, shepherd, potter. The title *King* is so pervasive that it required our focused attention in chapter 6. Most of these occupational titles, similar to the many terms that are noun forms of human activities—redeemer, helper, creator, protector, guide, keeper, deliverer, savior, maker—are gender-neutral, not only in the contemporary world but in biblical times as well. Deborah was a judge and a warrior. Rachel, like many

Bedouin young women then and now, was a shepherd. Unfortunately, biblical illiteracy and androcentric bias predispose our assemblies to assume that all human occupations except wetnurse are filled by males. The nineteenth-century cult of true womanhood, which urged all middle- and upper-class women to limit themselves to the occupation of homemaking, contributes to our hearing occupational titles as gender-specific. The first task before the church in using occupational metaphors is to avoid by anecdote, word choice, or accompanying illustration the implication that granting God an occupation construes God as male.

How is God a shepherd? Like Rachel in Genesis 29, God the shepherd daily rolls away the stone from the mouth of the well, so that the sheep may drink from the waters of life. Like David in 1 Samuel 17, God the shepherd rescues the flock from the mouths of lions and bears. Psalm 23, without male pronouns, celebrates this image. The metaphor of shepherd is archaic. Part of the wisdom of catechesis is to ascertain when and how often to use archaic images. The current popularity of world myths suggests that archaisms can hold contemporary people in a strong grip. Sometimes catechesis must include a context within which the metaphor can live.

God as judge is a recurring metaphor in the Psalms. According to Judges 4, in the days before Israel adopted the male monarchical structure of its neighbors, Deborah sat under the palm tree judging Israel. But the Bible introduces both competent and incompetent judges. One metaphor can offer only one facet of divine activity, one image more or less illuminating. Perhaps the less exotic the metaphor— we all know about both just and unjust judges—the more the church must say its No: "But God is not a judge." Not only is God not a judge because judges can be unjust; God does not easily fit the image of even a just judge. God is not seen vindicating the righteous and punishing the wicked. A judge who delays is not just; a judge who is inordinately merciful is not just.

The metaphor of judge illustrates yet another concern about anthropomorphisms for God. Although *judge* is not a dominant image of God in contemporary American Christianity, medieval church buildings suggest that it was, if not the sole image for the divine, at least an overwhelmingly significant one. The theological language of justification builds on the image of God as judge. Yet history illustrates the distortion that occurs when God becomes identified with only a single image. If God is only a stern judge, people search for a balance outside God, perhaps in Mary, to plead their causes. In our time some Christians choose the metaphor of God as friend. In some contexts a helpful corrective, the friend image, when standing alone, is finally a meager way to express divinity: *friend* is too defined by the self to convey the otherness of divinity. Every era of the church must stay alert to its dominant images, vigilant lest God become as small as the current human imagination.

The title *warrior* poses its own problems. Usually construed as male, although any careful reading of history proves otherwise,[11] the metaphor has been harshly criticized in recent decades as demeaning for the divine, its use glamorizing warfare and sanctifying violence. Hymnal committees have struggled with why warrior hymns are much loved and how many should be included in denominational collections. In Christian hymnody, the warrior is usually identified with Christ: see, for example, the nineteenth-century texts "Onward Christian Soldiers," "For All the Saints," and the twentieth-century text "Lift High the Cross."[12] Are the connotations of the metaphor *warrior* appropriate and helpful?

With such ambivalent metaphors, the yes-no-yes formula proves its usefulness. How is God a warrior? If one takes evil with deadly seriousness (which an optimistic humanism does not), one needs a God who leads the assault against the powers of the enemy.[13] When one is nearly overcome by evil, when one feels oneself abandoned in the fight for justice, the metaphor of God the warrior surprises with the promise of divine assistance. At the same time, no: God abhors violence; God's conquest is achieved by quite other than military might. Most surely, God is not to be commandeered as the general of a nation's armies in international disputes. What emerges, as with all metaphor, is a qualified yes. In some ways yes, in some ways no. As Paul Ricoeur wrote, "In metaphorical statements, the 'is' is both a literal 'is not' and a

---

11. See, for example, Antonia Fraser, *The Warrior Queens* (New York: Knopf, 1989).

12. *Lutheran Book Of Worship* (Minneapolis: Augsburg Publishing House, 1978), #509, #176, and #377.

13. Martin Luther King Jr., *Strength to Love* (Philadelphia: Fortress, 1963), 77–86.

metaphorical 'is like.'"[14] The question remains: How can this image, partial though it is, surprise the faithful with God's merciful might?

Hymn writers are offering yet other human metaphors. Peter Davidson's hymn "The Singer and the Song"[15] likens God to a singer whose song is divine love. Brian Wren has offered a variety of human titles, God as carpenter of the new creation[16] and as dancer, gambler, midwife, and weaver.[17] Sylvia Dunstan called Christ "lamb and shepherd, prince and slave."[18] These and many more such metaphors are needed, any one of which captures only a single facet of the divine brilliance. Only with a wealth of human images can Christians hope to reflect off one another's faces the mercy of God.

SEXUALLY EXPLICIT METAPHORS

The Christian tradition in art, catechesis, and homiletics has erroneously construed as sexually determined many anthropomorphisms that in fact are gender-neutral. A judge is not a male, or even a masculine, metaphor. Wisdom is not intrinsically female or feminine. Some anthropomorphisms, however, intentionally evoke sexually explicit human activities as the focus of the metaphor. We shall consider here the sexually explicit metaphors of lover, mother, and father, granting only several pages to what could occupy several books.

These words can have other than sexually explicit meanings. *Lover* can connote a close companion, with no sexual implications.[19] In many linguistic contexts, *mother* is an honorific granted a female primary caregiver. But it is the sexually explicit aspect of these words that interests us here, for explicit sexual activity always underlies the more abstract language of human love, creativity, and nurture. The contortions to which the tradition resorted in describing a virginal (all too often rendered as "pure") mother Mary only proves the rule that parental

14. Paul Ricoeur, "Biblical Hermeneutics," in *Semeia* 4, ed. John Dominic Crossan (Missoula, Mont.: Scholars Press, 1975), 88.

15. Peter Davidson, "The Singer and the Song," in *Songs for a Gospel People* (Winfield, British Columbia: Wood Lake Books, 1987), #54.

16. Brian Wren, in *Songs for a Gospel People*, #113.

17. Brian Wren, *Bring Many Names* (Carol Stream, Ill.: Hope Publishing Company, 1989), #2, #5, #20, and #25.

18. Sylvia Dunstan, "Christus Paradox," in *Songs for a Gospel People*, #64.

19. McFague, *Models of God*, 125–55.

language evokes and assumes sexual language. For this discussion, let us then define a lover as a partner chosen for sexual intimacy, a mother as a female who has given birth and continues to care for her child, and a father as a male who sired and continues to care for his child.

Religion ancient and modern is filled with mating deities. Still today in Hinduism sexual intercourse provides a dominant metaphor for the union of human with divine. In polytheism the deity may be the male or the female partner. In male monotheism the archetypal metaphor continued to function, but in only one direction. In the Bible God is the male partner and the chosen people the female. The Bible employs not only the contractual language of the covenant of marriage, but occasionally also the sexual imagery of passion and desire. The longing of God and the people is described with erotic overtones, although not with the explicit sexual iconography of other religious traditions.

The most significant use of erotic imagery in the Bible is in the Song of Songs, in which male and female lovers (nowhere identified as wed) are dynamically equal partners, both seeking and both attracting, both giving and both receiving. This love poem became an honored conceit in the Jewish tradition, functioning as a sustained metaphor of God's love for the chosen people. The church inherited this tradition. Enabled by an allegorical interpretation of such metaphors, especially Christian monasticism saw in the Song of Songs its most esoteric metaphor of the bond between Christ and the church.

The trajectory of this metaphor developed differently in Judaism than in Christianity. Judaism, assuming marriage for all the devout, was free to apply such love language to advice on sexual techniques in a lively marriage.[20] Medieval Christian celibate monasticism, on the other hand, while disparaging actual married lovemaking, idealized the sexual metaphor in inaccurate and disembodied speech in which the male was wholly active and the female wholly passive.[21] The male mystics took the metaphorical part of the passive female, and so the metaphor worked in opposition to the actual sexuality of the monk, with the result that the male monks avoided explicit bodily language in their increasingly fantastic reveries about their passion for God.

20. Judith Plaskow, *Standing Again at Sinai: Judaism from a Feminist Perspective* (San Francisco: Harper & Row, 1990), 161–62, 206–7.

21. E. Ann Matter, *The Voice of My Beloved: The Song of Songs in Western Medieval Christianity* (Philadelphia: University of Pennsylvania Press, 1990), 92–106.

After the twelfth century several changes occurred. Due to the growing attention to individual consciousness, the mystics increasingly applied the love language not to Christ and the church, but to God and the individual soul.[22] Female mystics, for whom the metaphor functioned more naturally, utilized more explicitly physical language than did the men. One nun after another, describing sexual ecstasy, filled her praise with descriptions of God's kiss on her lips, God's arms around her, God's power entering her, God's pressure against her body.[23] The later Middle Ages also saw an increase of interest in the humanity of Jesus, and this led some mystics to focus not on the mystical Risen Christ but on the physical body of Jesus. Margery Kempe, the mother of fourteen children, talked with remarkable realism about Jesus sitting by her bed, and because "her love and affection were fixed on the manhood of Christ," she responded to boys and men "as if she had seen Christ."[24]

As the women lauded Christ as their husband, however, they deprecated themselves. Powerful beliefs were operative here. Celibate women were likely to accept as biological fact the notion that females are wholly passive in intercourse. Late medieval androcentrism urged on women the belief that they were more fully and inescapably sexual, and thus further from God, than males. The woman's blood of menstruation and childbirth became a primary metaphor in an identification with the cross. Even maternal nursing was connected with suffering, since medieval science thought that mother's milk was derived from menstrual blood. Although the woman was a passive bleeding sufferer, so was there joy in union with God, the powerful creative actor.

Despite its long and problematic history in Christian tradition, erotic imagery is dormant in the contemporary church. The classic hymns that develop the lover image avoid explicit physicality. Philipp Nicolai's "Wake, O Wake, and Sleep No Longer" celebrates the marriage image, but as is common in Christian use, the nuptial imagery leads not to

---

22. Ibid., 111–23.

23. See, for example, Mechthild of Magdeburg, "The Flowing Light of the Godhead," in *Medieval Women's Visionary Literature*, ed. Elizabeth Alvilda Petroff (New York: Oxford University Press, 1986), 216. Also see Elizabeth Dreyer, *Passionate Women: Two Medieval Mystics* (New York: Paulist, 1989).

24. *The Book of Margery Kempe*, trans. B. A. Windeatt (New York: Viking Penguin, 1985), 42, 123.

a bedroom but to the Johannine banquet hall.[25] The Book of Revelation intentionally breaks the image; one does not conjure up erotic feelings about a feast presided over by the Lamb. Brilliantly, the image has said both Yes and No to marriage with God. Some recent hymns using romantic language sound adolescent, as if believers are teenagers gazing at a movie star's picture, rather than vintage lovers sharing the ecstacy, the heartache, even the quotidian, of genuine human lovemaking.

It is odd that as our culture comes to worship sexual union as one of its highest values, the church avoids sexual language in metaphor for God. Perhaps the celibate bias of Roman Catholicism and the Victorian cult of true womanhood, both of which sidestep explicit sexual language, still dictate the church's essentially conservative religious language. It may be time to reexplore the language of God as lover, both the male lover filling the believer with divine power, and the female lover embracing the individual's naked aloneness, both seeking, both finding, both needing, both giving, the two interlocked toward their creative future. Yet any use of the lover metaphor must include a resounding No: God has no beard, no breasts; God is not a deity mating with devotees to bear life; human beings are not equal to God, as one hopes human lovers are to one another.

Although the church continues hesitant about God as lover, overkill of God as father has led to many calls for God to be mother.[26] God as nursing mother has been an important image for male celibates, who found it more amenable when drinking from the breasts of God to be children than lovers.[27] That God like a mother contains us in a womb of mercy; that God labors to bring forth both us and our salvation; that God nurses us with divine life: these biblical metaphors must be, and are being, revived. Recent denominational hymnals and service orders include examples of the metaphor of God as mother.[28] Too often,

25. "Wake, O Wake, and Sleep No Longer," trans. Christopher Idle, in *Worship*, 3d ed. (Chicago: GIA Publications, 1986), #371.

26. See, for example, McFague, *Models of God*, 97–123, and Johnson, *She Who Is*, 170–87.

27. Sister Ritamary Bradley, "Patristic Background of the Motherhood Similitude in Julian of Norwich," in *Christian Scholar's Review* 8 (1978): 101–13.

28. For some examples, see *The United Methodist Hymnal* (Nashville: United Methodist Publishing House, 1989) #66, #111; *The Presbyterian Hymnal: Hymns, Psalms, and Spiritual Songs* (Louisville: Westminster/John Knox Press, 1990), #323, #523; *The United Methodist Book of Worship* (Nashville: United Methodist Publishing House, 1992), #439, #586.

theologians have flailed against language of God as mother as a heretical attack on the Trinity. It is time for the church to use the mother image, and in contexts other than prayers for newborns. Women, however, must be attentive to what is involved when they propose motherhood as the preeminent divine metaphor. Undoubtedly the image functions differently for those women who are mothers than for those who are not.

As with all metaphors, the use of God-as-mother brings both possibilities and pitfalls. We know this metaphor perhaps most evocatively in the writing of Julian of Norwich.[29] But underlying Julian's praise of Christ as her mother is the image of the mother as passive bleeding sufferer, the one who as Aristotle taught has more sexuality than a man has, the gender more readily acquainted with death. Because woman was thought to have more to do with bodies than was man, Julian sees in Christ the mother the bodiliness of God. In Julian we are reminded that the sexual imagery of the one bearing and nursing is never far from the cultural stereotype of the one who suffers, and that while both are true of God, it is not clear that both are true of mothers.

Other caveats exist. Not all women are mothers. Not all mothers are nurturing. Not all mothers can recall their experience in positive light; for some mothers, childbirth generates their deepest unhappiness and child-rearing is despised. Not all people have reason to honor their mothers. Mothers can clutch their children to death perhaps more forcefully than can fathers. We must guard against rhapsodic praise of the mother. One linguistic theory suggests that males have defined *motherhood* as a wholly positive term, making nuanced talk about mothering difficult.[30] We must remember that childbirth has killed many women, and becoming a mother is the most natural instinct of which females throughout the animal kingdom are capable. Motherhood is no key to divine power, no univocal symbol of creativity.

An ethical issue must also be raised. For many millennia in the West, the male was thought to be the primary progenitor, and in many places the male legally owned his offspring. We cannot merely turn the record over by suggesting that the female is the sole parent. To fill religious language with imagery of the mother who in her own

29. Juliana of Norwich, chapters 58–61, in *Revelations of Divine Love*.

30. Dale Spender, *Man Made Language* (London: Routledge & Kegan Paul, 1980), 54–58.

power conceives and by her own resources bears and nurtures her children distorts the truth of human sexuality. The brilliant contribution of Christian ethics to sexual issues, not yet fully explored, is that the sexual couple together owns its sexuality in which two halves have become one, and that the couple cooperates in the nurture of any children, who belong not to either parent but to themselves and to God. Neither androcentric nor gynocentric language about sexuality is finally particularly Christian.

What is so intriguing about God-the-mother language is that it has become far more physically explicit than God-the-father language ever was. Catechesis, mystagogy, homiletics, and hymnody now praise God's womb and breasts, although the Christian tradition never praised God's penis or testicles. In describing God's "body," Christian hymnody traditionally reached for androgyny by evoking neither female breasts nor the male chest, but a masculine breast. There was also the image of "the bosom of Abraham." God's beard was pictured but in Christianity was never the focus of meditation and praise.[31] The age-old conundrum persists, that in the West female embodiment has been linguistically and socially acceptable but male embodiment has not. Much in our culture is accustomed to praising the female nude yet acts offended by the male nude. If Christians choose to celebrate female body language in praise of the divine, they must discover how to do so for male language as well. If not, Christian men will find themselves in the same situation as the medieval celibates, whose system of metaphor arose out of a fantasy that in fact denegrated their sexuality.

In Christian metaphor, *father* is used almost exclusively to evoke patriarchial authority, rather than to suggest a sexual imagery of fathering. The problematic description of God in Hebrews 12 explicitly connects the father with the harsh disciplinarian. Although historically the metaphor of father comes into religion as a way to designate the origin of the king, in Judaism and Christianity *father* is a behavior pattern, not a biological image. Perhaps it is because father-language came into the church via the myth of the crown that it connotes dominance rather than familial fathering. The tradition offers little

31. This contrasts with the medieval Jewish Zohar, which includes extended contemplation of the beard of God: see *The Wisdom of the Kabbalah*, intro. by Dagobert D. Runes (New York: Wisdom Library, 1957), 44–84.

exposition of the nurturing image of "your heavenly Father" in the Sermon on the Mount. Christian theologians have always vociferously denied that the language of God's fatherhood of Jesus had anything to do with divine sexuality, and this denial was demonstrated by refusing metaphoric talk of God's paternity. The continuous references to God as father in the tradition are in fact no proof that the metaphor of father has been explored by Christian imagination and shaped by the gospel.

As the church explores sexually explicit metaphors for God, an ongoing and resounding "No!" to such sexual metaphors must be heard. Sexuality is a method by which beings that will die are reproduced. Human sexuality is the process that creates life in the face of death, both by engendering new human beings and by fostering love between sexual partners. While believers praise God for conceiving, bearing, nursing, and rearing them, the church has not, for good reasons, seen any truth in language about God's sexual organs or actions. Rather, Scripture and hymnody have freely alluded to God's eyes, ears, voice, face, arms, and hands, all gender-neutral anthropomorphisms. When Christians use explicit sexual metaphors for God, they must strenuously work to keep the metaphors alive, or the image quickly hardens into one of nature, not of mercy. Christian faith maintains that God acts counter to the uncaring and natural order of creation. While it is true that the church has to the world's peril neglected to honor the earth, monotheism understands that God is other than Mother Earth and that God's merciful salvation is beyond an everlasting mating. We must always remember the No. As soon as we speak, we negate. God is lover, mother, father; God is not lover, mother, father.

In the Roman world of the first century, the metaphor of God as patriarch was commonplace. Although he may not have been the only visionary to alter the metaphor, Jesus is remembered as having added a new story onto the old foundation. The title *Abba* caught the imagination of some early Christians, who heard in its variation on regular religion a new song of mercy. The God known through Jesus was praised for establishing new frontiers, for the poor in a world of oppressors, for the outsiders in an exclusive religious tradition, for women in an androcentric culture. A powerful religious metaphor can radically reorient religion, turning the homage of sky-dwelling deities who act like irresponsible humanoids into a compassionate way of life for human beings among whom God is incarnate. The new thing in Christianity is not anthropomorphisms for God, but the incarnation of God within humanity. Thus in every use of anthropomorphism, Christians must be sure that their language describes not the old ruin of religion but the amazing city of God.

nine

OBJECTIFYING METAPHORS FOR GOD

Anthropomorphisms are not the only technique available to the church for metaphoric descriptions of God. John Donne exults in the various options the Scriptures teach:

> My God, my God, thou art a direct God. . . . But thou art a figurative, a metaphorical God too: a God in whose words there is such a height of figures, such voyages, such peregrinations to fetch remote and precious metaphors, such extensions, such spreadings, such curtains of allegories, such third heavens of hyperboles, so harmonious elocutions, so retired and so reserved expressions, so commanding persuasions, so persuading commandments . . . thou art the dove that flies.[1]

In turning from anthropomorphic to objective metaphors for God, we discover that the greatest danger no longer threatens: although calling God a judge suggests to many people that God is literally a judge, and although some people take comfort in imaging God to be like humans, no one in calling God a dove confuses the deity with a bird. When God is called after an object, the metaphor tends to remain a metaphor. In *The Donkey's Dream*, Barbara Helen Berger's children's story of the birth of Jesus, the donkey imagines that on his back he is carrying a city, a ship, a fountain, and a rose.[2] These objective metaphors praise aspects of the mission of the coming infant, but the images remain metaphors, without pretending to become descriptions of what the incarnate God actually is.

---

1. John Donne, *Devotions upon Emergent Occasions* (Ann Arbor: University of Michigan Press, 1959), 124.

2. Barbara Helen Berger, *The Donkey's Dream* (New York: Philomel Books, 1985).

FREEDOM FOR METAPHOR

The psalter teaches Christians freedom in address to God and inspires the metaphoric pen. God is like natural phenomena, the sun in the sky and, conversely, the shade protecting us from sun. God is the mountain range that surrounds the chosen people's city forever. God is identified with the products of human life: God is a tower and a cup. In Psalm 18, God is strength, rock, fortress, shield, a stronghold, a volcano, an earthquake, and a hailstorm, as well as the commander of armies. These archaic metaphors have remained accessible over the centuries to enrich Christian prayer.

Other metaphors in the psalms are somewhat alien. God is our "portion," that is, the section of homeland promised to our particular tribe, our future security. Such a metaphor, if literalized in contemporary politics, can suggest realities the metaphor was never meant to convey. God is also "the horn of my salvation," a phrase scholars debate. Perhaps the huge phallic horn from ancient religion survives in this poem, as in the design of the altar, as a metaphor of masculine strength, as if God were a male animal overpowering a rival; perhaps the ancient connotation has been tamed by becoming the musical instrument of the shofar, the animal horn that called out Israel's salvation. When the liturgy incorporates such obscure ancient metaphors, appropriate translation or helpful contextualization is often required for meaningful prayer.

Yet even a straightforward metaphor is never simple. How is light a metaphor for God? Just as we saw with anthropomorphisms, God is and is not like light. The mystics remind us, lest we divinize the sun or think to have described God fully, that God is also the darkness of unknowing. Pseudo-Dionysius writes of the Godhead, "It is not immovable, moving, or at rest. It has no power, it is not power, nor is it light. . . . It is not kingship. It is not wisdom. . . . Darkness and light, error and truth—it is none of these" . . . but "is free of every limitation, beyond every limitation."[3] It is hoped that this insight of the mystical *via negativa*, far from inhibiting the use of metaphors, frees Christians for more creativity.

---

3. Pseudo-Dionysius, "The Divine Names," in *Pseudo-Dionysius: The Complete Words*, trans. Colm Luibheid (New York: Paulist, 1987), 131.

The tradition presents examples of praise of an endlessly faceted divinity. Symeon the New Theologian praises "this Unique Being" as:

> light and peace and joy, life, food and drink, clothing, a robe, a tent and a divine dwelling, the East, the resurrection, repose and a bath, fire, water, river, source of life and a flowing stream, bread and wine, the new delight of believers, the banquet, the pleasure which we enjoy in a mystical way, sun, indeed, without any setting, star always shining, lamp that burns inside the dwelling of the soul.[4]

Gertrud the Great writes praise to the "eternal solstice, safe dwelling, place containing all pleasure, heavenly garden of everlasting delights flowing with streams of pleasures beyond price."[5] The church's classic hymnody is replete with such objective metaphors. Thomas Aquinas's eucharistic hymn lauds Christ as the mother pelican, who, when her mate murders her offspring, revives them with her own blood.[6] Philipp Nicolai's "Wie schön leuchtet" praises the divine as morning star, light, tree, treasure, crown, beginning, and end.[7] Recent hymnody explodes with objective metaphors. For Miriam Therese Winter, God is wellspring of wisdom, dawn of a new day, and garden of grace.[8] For R. Deane Postlethwaite, God is the mother eagle who pushes the eaglet out of the nest to teach it to fly, but soars underneath to catch it with her open wings if it "flutter helplessly."[9] In one hymn, Thomas Troeger evokes forty metaphors, including rock, cloud, fortress, fountain, shelter, light, root, vine, well, storm, stillness, thunder, tempest, whirlwind, and fire.[10] It is instructive that of the seven Advent "O" antiphons

---

4. Symeon the New Theologian, *Hymns of Divine Love*, trans. George A. Maloney, S.J. (Denville, N.J.: Dimension Books, n.d.), 233–34.

5. Gertrud the Great, *The Herald of God's Loving-Kindness*, trans. Alexandra Barratt (Kalamazoo, Mich.: Cistercian Publications, 1991), 123.

6. Thomas Aquinas, "Godhead Here in Hiding," in *The Collegeville Hymnal*, ed. Edward J. McKenna (Collegeville, Minn.: Liturgical Press, 1990), #368.

7. Philipp Nicolai, "O Morning Star," in *Lutheran Book of Worship* (Minneapolis: Augsburg, 1978), #76.

8. Miriam Therese Winter, "Wellspring of Wisdom," in *The United Methodist Hymnal* (Nashville: United Methodist Publishing House, 1989), #506.

9. R. Deane Postlethwaite, "The Care the Eagle Gives Her Young," in *The United Methodist Hymnal*, #118.

10. Thomas Troeger, "Source and Sovereign, Rock and Cloud," in *The United Methodist Hymnal*, #113.

from the ninth century, three are objective: root of Jesse's tree and key of David, as well as dayspring, prayed on the day of the winter solstice itself.

The Gospel of John turns the psalm's pattern of objective metaphors for God to Christ and the sacraments. If God is a fountain of life, Christ is the living water, which the church encounters in baptism. If God is food for the people, Christ is the bread of life, which the Christian receives in the Eucharist. If God is light in the darkness, Christ is the light of the world, whom Christians celebrate annually at the Paschal Vigil and recall each night at evening prayer. John plays with the Israelite metaphor of God as the people's shepherd to show all its facets: Christ is the gatekeeper, but also the gate itself, and the sacramental community the enclosed herd. The Jewish tradition symbolized the connection between God and the chosen people by the lamb: provided for the people by God, the lamb was given back to God and thus became a sign of both God's mercy and the people's faith. In John the lamb becomes one of the central metaphors for Christ, the personified connection between God and the people. Christ is not only the gate guarding the flock but also the lamb itself snatched by the wolf. A great poet can sing many variations on a single metaphor. The church's goal should be that at least these many connotations be available to the faithful during the singing of "Lamb of God."

Feminist Christians have reason to rejoice at this recent proliferation of ancient and innovative metaphors. Objective metaphors present by their very diversity an antidote to the monolithic masculine bias of much anthropomorphism. A wealth of images celebrates an endlessly faceted God, a God not wholly contained by doctrine, a God beyond human categories, yet a God whom we can glimpse in terms of the common objects of our lives. It is illuminating that in describing the Spirit of God, increasingly important for feminist Christian spirituality, tradition has usually avoided anthropomorphism and chosen instead objectification, the Spirit as dove, fire, wind, oil, fountain, light.

RESTRICTIONS ON METAPHOR

Although liturgical language is metaphoric, the liturgy is not in fact poetry, especially as contemporary Western literature practices poetry. Western poetry of this century tends to be highly personal expression.

Its metaphors are shared more or less by persons of similar life experience, and its effect is laid on the reader or hearer just as a performance
is presented before an audience. While in some cultures, for example,
preliterate ones, poetry was a communal expression of the people's
myths and poems were recited in participatory assemblies of the entire
community, this is not the case in contemporary Western culture. For
us, poetry is usually encountered on the page, not in the ear. Usually
its syntax requires careful attention and its metaphors demand analysis.
Only a highly selective group of people can be bonded together by a
poetry reading.

Thus in the liturgy not any old metaphor, or any new metaphor,
will do. Liturgy is not an individual's performance laid before others;
nor is it a collection of texts of self-expression. Liturgical language
takes as its model not a Pulitzer prize-winning poem but the prologue
of John: it is speech that the baptized community already shares.
Liturgical language bonds together the worshiping people because it
is already their speech. Liturgical metaphors change over the decades.
The texts, hymns, and prayers have evolved over the centuries and
must continue to evolve. But innovations in liturgical speech must
take care that novel metaphors not fragment the assembly, but unite
it. Liturgical imagery is not idiosyncratic but communal. Many people
just beginning liturgical experimentation turn to modern poetry to
enhance the service. This practice usually develops one of two ways:
either the liturgy mutates into poetry readings, or the assembly
pulls back from such personal expression into the metaphors of
corporate faith.

The primary source for liturgical metaphor is the Bible. One definition of Christian liturgy is the communal celebration of biblical
metaphors. The new light of creation, the Red Sea, the living water,
manna in the desert, the body of Christ, the Garden of Eden, the city
of God: such images as these constitute the church's core vocabulary,
the root metaphors of its communal speech. The fact of an increasing
biblical illiteracy must be met not by abandoning scriptural references
in the liturgy, for this would deny the liturgy its building blocks,
excise its very backbone. Rather, the churches must intensify oppor-
tunities for biblical study. Children and adults at all levels can be

encouraged in Bible study. [11] Creative home learning aids, from children's Bible story books to Advent Jesse trees, can be made available so that not only Sunday morning but one's entire life can be expresssed by core Christian metaphors. [12] Although biblical literacy will mark only a minority of the population, worshiping Christians will be part of that minority.

Some liturgical metaphors are not originally Jewish or Christian but arose in ancient human symbolization of the divine. Thus they connect Christians to people throughout time and space. The mythological image of the sea monster gives a metaphor for chaos both inside and out; the archetypal image of flowing water is used as a metaphor of divine love; the classical philosophical image of the Logos becomes a metaphor for the incarnation. The natural world gives abundant metaphors for God: the dove that flies, the earthquake, the winter solstice. Literal statements tend to narrow, but metaphoric images to broaden: such multivalent metaphors can have meaning for people of different ages and different life situations who come to the worship in divergent moods and with diverse needs. Take, for example, the metaphor *heaven*. In the phrase "Heaven help us," what does *heaven* mean to suggest about God? Originally the word meant the natural sky, the vast space beyond the earth; in mythology heaven is the realm of beings greater than humans; in religion it has meant the place where human life is extended beyond its boundary of death. Heaven is the black of night, the countless stars, the blue expanse, the matrix of hurricanes, the abode of angels: a multivalent metaphor for God. And if that is not enough, Cyril of Jerusalem instructed his catechumens that heaven, which is the abode of God, is in fact the eucharistic assembly. [13]

THE METAPHOR OF THE TREE OF LIFE

An objective metaphor for the divine whose time has come is the tree of life. It is important first to clarify why the symbol of the tree functions ambivalently in the Bible. The Hebrew Scriptures contain diatribes

11. One example of a children's biblical liturgical guide is Gail Ramshaw, *Sunday Morning* (Chicago: Liturgy Training Publications, 1993).

12. An example of such helps is Gertrude Mueller Nelson, *To Dance with God* (New York: Paulist, 1986).

13. Cyril of Jerusalem, *Lectures on the Christian Sacraments* (Crestwood, N.Y.: St. Vladimir's Seminary Press, 1977), 75.

against worship in a grove of trees and specific condemnations of the Asherah pole, especially when it periodically found its way into the temple precincts. The reason for this rejection is clear: the dominant Canaanite goddess, Asherah, was symbolized by a tree or a branchless pole, which served as a reminder of the fertility of the land that Asherah guaranteed.[14] Egyptian, Babylonian, and Canaanite art and cult objects all contain images of a tree as the depiction either of the goddess or of the deity incarnate in the monarch. Contemporary scholars postulate that the prophets inveigh more specifically against Baal than Asherah because although the god Baal was replaced by YHWH, the cult of Asherah may have remained more or less in place. Some evidence suggests that among the less-than-orthodox, Asherah was merely transferred over to be consort of YHWH.[15]

It is likely that the story in Numbers 21 of Moses raising a serpent on a pole to effect the people's healing contains a memory of Canaanite goddess veneration, in which the serpent, an ancient symbol of fecundity, was often depicted in a tree to symbolize feminine divine power. Yet according to the story as recorded by the Israelites, it was YHWH who commanded the Canaanite-like religious devotion involving the serpent. The Hebrew tradition understood itself to be initially nomadic, and so its deity was not grounded in a particular land mass but was transcendent to the earth and manifested not in the soil and its fertility but throughout the progress of human events. The tree has been cut down and a roadway built. Thus the Torah recalls veneration of the goddess's tree but circumcises the memory.

In spite of the rejection of Asherah's tree, the Scriptures begin and end with the tree as a symbol of God's life. In Genesis 2–3, the tree of life is prominent in the created paradise, and eating from it grants immortality. The immoral, mortal creatures are denied its fruits. In Revelation 22, the tree with its twelve kinds of fruits and its leaves "for the healing of the nations" is a primary image of shared bliss in the perfected city of God. The tree recurs throughout the Bible as an archetypal metaphor for the good. In the Psalms and in Jesus' parables,

14. See John Day, "Asherah in the Hebrew Bible and Northwest Semitic Literature," *Journal of Biblical Literature* 105/3 (1986): 385–408.

15. See, for example, Mark S. Smith, *The Early History of God: Yahweh and the Other Deities in Ancient Israel* (San Francisco: Harper & Row, 1990), 80–99.

the fruitful tree is a metaphor for those who live the godly life. Sirach 24 describes Lady Wisdom herself as the tree of life. In Ezekiel 17 and 31 and in Romans 11, the tree, known in the ancient Near East as a symbol for a mighty nation and its ruler, becomes a symbol for God's lowly people. Early Christians recognized the metaphoric potential of the tree image by claiming in the earliest level of proclamation (Gal. 3:13; Acts 10:39-40) that Christ was hanged on a tree.

The cross as the tree of life has stayed alive within the Christian tradition. By the fourth century, the identification of the cross as the tree of life was popularized through the legend of Constantine's mother, Helena, having exhumed the true cross and discovering that its fragments still could raise the dead. When in Poitiers the nuns of Queen Radegund's convent acquired a fragment of this wood, their chaplain and poet, Venantius Fortunatus, penned the masterpieces known as "Sing, my tongue, the glorious battle" and "The royal banners forward go,"[16] both of which praise the cross as the beauteous tree of life. The kontakia of the Eastern church[17] and the eighth-century Anglo-Saxon poem "The Dream of the Rood"[18] describe the cross as the tree of life.

Medieval churches are filled with Christianized trees of life. Eastern churches depicted in icons the legend of the discovery of the true cross. The Jesse tree, an image recurring in European stained-glass windows, places the ancestors of Christ on ascending branches of a tree rooted in the body of sleeping Jesse and topped with Mary holding the baby Jesus. In variations of this image, the disciples or theologians or the Christian virtues are fruits on the branches. In some depictions an intertwining flowing vine extends from a central cross. Sometimes the tree features in another metaphor: for example, the pelican feeding her offspring from her breast is nested in a tree, or Jonah pulls himself out of the fish's mouth by grabbing on to a tree. The nineteenth-century Shakers, who believed that they were already enjoying the kingdom of God thanks to both Jesus Christ and Mother Ann, used the tree of

16. Venantius Fortunatus, in *Lutheran Book of Worship*, #118, #125.

17. Romanos, "On the Victory of the Cross," in *Kontakia of Romanos, Byzantine Melodist*, trans. Marjorie Carpenter (Columbia: University of Missouri Press, 1970), 1:230–38.

18. For a liturgical translation, see Gail Ramshaw, " 'The Dream of the Rood': A Translation," in *Worship: Searching for Language* (Washington, D.C.: Pastoral Press, 1988), 17–22.

life as the central symbol for the divine life their community shared.[19] The motif lives into this century, for example, in the much-reproduced stained-glass windows of Louis Tiffany, Frank Lloyd Wright, Marc Chagall, and Henri Matisse. Several recently published hymns recall the tree of life,[20] and the current Episcopal lectionary includes the image in all three cycles of the sixth Sunday of Easter.

The tree of life as metaphor for God would serve the contemporary church well, for several reasons. First, such use would help reverse the church's despicable pattern of devaluing the created world. While Christianity maintains that salvation is not a phenomenon of nature, Christians ought to honor creation as a gift of divine goodness and a sign of divine life. Those in the ecological movement have made use of the tree as a transnational symbol of the organic fecundity of nature. Christians can use this popular image of life to proclaim that they find this tree of organic and beautiful fecundity especially in God.

Further, the tree connects Christians with many of the world's religious traditions. The menorah of Judaism, the tree pattern on an Islamic prayer carpet, the kadamba tree of Krishna in Hinduism, the bodhi tree in Buddhism, the ash tree of Norse mythology, the tree with its five birds in Egyptian iconography, the Mohawk pine tree, the Navaho cornstalk, and the Lakota tree of life at the center of the world are only a few of the trees next to which the Christian cross must stand in dialogue.[21] The Gbaya Christians in Cameroon have continued ritual use of their traditional healing tree, the soré, and in their Christian liturgy now praise Christ as the true soré tree.[22] The church could thus continue the pattern seen in the use of the Christmas tree: some ancient peoples decorated their homes with evergreens at the time of the winter

---

19. Edward Deming Andrews and Faith Andrews, *Visions of the Heavenly Sphere: A Study in Shaker Religious Art* (Charlottesville: University Press of Virginia, 1969).

20. Kiraly Imre von Pecselyi, "There in God's Garden," trans. Eric Routley, in *A New Hymnal for Colleges and Schools*, ed. Jeffrey Rowthorn and Russell Schulz-Widmar (New Haven: Yale University Press, 1992), #257; Marty Haugen, "Tree of Life," in *Mass of Creation* (Chicago: GIA Publications, 1984).

21. For many more examples, see Roger Cook, *The Tree of Life* (New York: Thames and Hudson, 1988), and Nathaniel Altman, *Sacred Trees* (San Francisco: Sierra Club Books, 1994).

22. Thomas G. Christensen, *An African Tree of Life* (Maryknoll, N.Y.: Orbis Books, 1990).

solstice to invoke the birth of the sun, and Christians adopted this practice and identified the tree with Christ.

Perhaps the main reason for use of the tree of life as a symbol for God is its multivalence. It is easy for the evergreen or the fruitful tree to serve as a metaphor of divine blessing. But drought comes; volcanos bury forests; harvest time yields nothing for children to eat. A flowering tree is not profound enough to image that mercy of God quite beyond the natural order. The Christian tradition, however, offers not only the fertile tree in the garden of God, but also the crossbeam on the pole stuck into Golgotha's hill. God is experienced not only in the twelve fruits and in healing leaves, but also in the blood flowing from the world's misery and injustice. The Christian hope is that the tree of death, always among us, can become the tree of life. As Jesus' parable in Mark 4 tells it, the mustard seed yields that archetypal tree of life immense enough for all the birds of the air to nest in: however, as Jesus' hearers knew, the mustard shrub is an unimpressive annual, a "tree" that is always dying. Not so much a king on a throne, but a tree that knows death and grants life: for the community of the faithful, such a tree can be Christ on the cross and the Creator of the universe, all in one.

In Douglas Wood's children's book *Old Turtle*, all of creation is arguing about the nature of God.[23] The star claims that "God is a twinkling and a shining, far, far away." The antelope insists God "is a runner, swift and free." "She is a great tree," murmurs the willow. "No, He is a river," thunders the waterfall. Finally all of creation looks beyond itself. Only when the stone can feel God's breath in the wind and the ocean know God among the snowcapped peaks does the knowledge of God begin. The most important gift that objective metaphors for God give us is the reminder that, just as God is not human, we are not God. In too much of human life, we worship ourselves. Christian liturgy gives us the opportunity to worship not ourselves, but God, and objective metaphors may help us keep the two distinct.

---

23. Douglas Wood, *Old Turtle*, illus. Cheng-Khee Chee (Duluth, Minn.: Pfeifer-Hamilton Publishers, 1992).

ten

VERBS FOR A LIVELY GOD

When we use the word *God* to mean the fulfillment of our desires, we have grounded religion in human need. What is the human problem? We express our need, and the religion conveys the divine power we seek. Is the human condition the guilt of sin, the terror of death, the agony of injustice, the pain of disease, the disorder of psychic chaos? No different than if one tribe needs rain and another sunshine, different understandings of the human problem construct different deities, because the god has been shaped by the need. If God is shaped by my need, and I have not identified any serious need in my life, having no need of God, I need not bother with religion.

While Judaism and Christianity affirm that God answers human need, they have sought to counter this typical religious pattern by maintaining that faith begins not in human need but in divine action. God created the world, not to respond to human need, but to express divine love. The activity of God precedes all and sustains all, and only as we find ourselves distant from our grounding in God do we discover our need. Religion is a response to God's action; we start the circle of human need and divine power with God.

A GOD WHO ACTS

The Scriptures record the believers' perception that God pursues humankind: God calls and leads, forgives and restores. In the Exodus 3 story of the burning bush, God is revealed with a verbal name I AM, as the deity who will act to save the chosen people. According to the Scriptures, believers know God not out of philosophical speculation into the divine being but in reception of and reflection on God's actions on their behalf. Abstract theorizing about God's essence can get far off the Christian track, for biblical data about God is about divine activity on humanity's behalf.[1] Abraham Heschel states that God is the one who acts to effect justice, and that what it means to be created in the divine image is that humns are created to act, like God, "in relieving affliction, in granting joy."[2]

The Psalms are filled with praise to a God who acts. Psalm 65 states, "By awesome deeds you answer us with deliverance," and goes on to praise God's actions in nature: God establishes the mountains, silences the seas, waters the earth. Psalm 104 includes not only realistic descriptions of the universe, such as "You cause the grass to grow," but also mythological claims: "You ride on the wings of the wind." Psalm 147 contains one verb after another: God lifts up, casts down, covers, prepares, gives, grants, fills, sends, scatters, hurls, declares. The detailed Israelite narratives in Psalms 105–107 and 135–136 attest that God acts also in human history. Other psalms recognize that this God, like other deities, will also answer the needs of one's personal life. The God who protects, saves, and delivers also cures illness (Psalm 30) and forgives sin (Psalm 51).

Christians believe that God is seen not only in actions of majestic power. By becoming incarnate in Christ and in the community, God acts also in human form, being born, eating, dying. Christ heals and forgives, preaches and serves, living as one of us. Christian ethics proceeds from the incarnation: inspired by God's transforming deeds among human beings, Christians can engage in lives of transformation. God not only sends rain and tempest but in Christ and in the community joins the faithful at the dinner table. Thus divine action is extended throughout all human life.

Secular culture resists belief in a God who acts. Deism, so influential in American philosophical thought, while believing that God acted once to create the world, maintained that God was now in retirement and that it was superstitious to hope for continuing divine intervention.

1. Catherine Mowry LaCugna, *God for Us: The Trinity and Christian Life* (San Francisco: HarperCollins, 1991), argues that the Trinity is best understood as God *pro nobis*, not God *in se*.

2. Abraham Joshua Heschel, *God in Search of Man* (New York: Harper & Row, 1955), 290.

Current scientific bias trains us to comprehend and quantify natural forces so as to locate any agency other than the divine as the operative force in the universe and human life. Believers adopt such secular stance when their intercessory prayers wholly replace petitions which plead for God to act with suggestions that humanity act in salvific ways. A bid to "help us to realize that we must feed the poor" is a noble sentiment in a secular age, but it is not the prayer of a countercultural faith which believes that not only the community, but the very God, can act to create justice in the world. The community of faith is the assembly that witnesses to God's verbs. God has acted, is acting, will act. Christians stand in the tradition of those who saw God acting, even in those places that the faithful were not acting.

VERBS BEYOND GENDER

Does praise of God for divine action necessarily imply gendered activity? What action if anything, beyond the tasks of procreation, is distinctive to each human sex? In the terms of this chapter, which verbs are, or ought to be, or ought not to be gender-specific? Considerable discussion has taken place both inside and around the feminist movement concerning gendered activities. The nature-versus-nurture debate inquires whether any such differences are essential to gender, rooted in biological destiny, or whether they are socially constructed through cultural formation. The liberal-versus-cultural schools of feminism debate whether society thrives under equal treatment of the sexes or whether distinctive gender patterns mark a healthy culture.[3] The categories *maximizer* and *minimizer* do not presuppose agreement on the complex issues of biological, psychological, or social origins and tendencies of gender, but merely seek to distinguish those who maximize difference between the sexes from those who do not.[4] Thus this study of language for God, not the place to argue these many questions, benefits by using the labels *maximizer* and *minimizer*.

Western Christianity has developed so as to maximize. Ancient Hebrew religion, similar to many primary religions, was marked by

3. Josephine Donovan, *Feminist Theory: The Intellectual Traditions of American Feminism* (New York: Ungar, 1986), 3, 31.

4. Maggie McFadden, "Anatomy of Difference: Toward a Classification of Feminist Theory," in *Women's Studies International Forum* 7/6 (1984): 495–504.

thorough gender distinction, in which the people's actions toward one another and God's actions toward an individual were contingent on biology. Greek philosophical thought, one of the pillars of Western civilization and pervasive in Western language, delineated clear distinctions observed in males and females that followed logically from biological difference.[5] Males, whose sperm was thought to contain all that is essentially human in reproduction, were dominant, more active, and more rational. Women, as passive receivers who embodied nature, were submissive. Thus a correlation between male activity and divine action seemed apparent to many Christian minds, and stereotypical female behavior served as a model for the role of the receptive church or the submissive Christian. Even when science demonstrated that the ancient world had its reproductive biology all wrong, many of the old claims persisted.

Many human behavioral studies demonstrate that gender distinctions are indeed pervasive—that girls play different games than boys during recess, that girls and women talk with different linguistic patterns than do boys and men, that young people demonstrate sex differences in national tests. These popular examples suggest that gender distinction is, if not prescriptive, at least descriptive. Maximizers in the feminist movement cite such data but reverse the traditional valuing. While males' thought may be more logical than females', the contextual pattern of females is valued as better for the universe. For males to be less emotional is judged unhealthy. This pattern of thought was popularized by nineteenth-century Romanticism, the idea of separate spheres and the cult of true womanhood. Males, whose tasks brought them daily into the wicked world, were assumed to have lost their natural connections to God, but women's gender-distinctive tasks allowed them continued closeness to religion. Thus Friedrich Schleiermacher lauds women's behavior as the more wholesome for human community and more attuned to the divine, depicting Sophia as a prepubescent girl enjoying most direct access to God.[6] Carl Jung stood in this tradition, urging the androcentric West to rediscover its anima and

<hr>

5. Aristotle, *Generation of Animals*, Loeb Classical Library 13 (Cambridge, Mass.: Harvard University Press, 1979), 113, 183–87.

6. Friedrich Schleiermacher, *Christmas Eve: Dialogue on the Incarnation*, trans. Terrence N. Tice (Richmond: John Knox Press, 1967), 51–57.

integrate supposed masculine and feminine actions into a wholistic individuation.[7]

This distinction between male and female behavior fills the current discussion of God-language. Traditional liturgical prayer, in which God conquers chaos, rules the world, judges human sin, battles against evil, and fathers a son, is seen as drawing solely from the male side of a double-column list of anthropomorphized divine activity.[8] The language of many new prayers draws from the other column: God births the universe, nurtures the world, guides humans into truth, encircles the community, mothers a people. Some feminist Christians urge a balance between male and female verbs, while others more radically advocate a complete sex change into the divine feminine—if not for all of Christianity, at least as a fervent corrective to the church's continuing androcentrism. Some prominent proponents of these positions are celibate religious, who, living lives more sex-segregated than the general population, are personally predisposed to accept gender distinctions as foundational, and whose countercultural stance helps them to value so-called feminine behavior as the more godly.[9]

The widening of divine activity in Christian speech is not only welcome but also absolutely necessary. A god who acts in only a few ways, a god whose activity is limited by impoverished faith or imagination, is a god in decline, ready to go into retirement. While scientific knowledge seeks wholly natural explanations for everything, so that nothing is left for God to do, the current doubling and tripling of divine verbs is an encouraging sign of lively faith. Not only is there a God, but a God who acts, in a pattern more faithful than we can remember, in ways more imaginative than we had thought. After all, the Scriptures teach that God began action, all of it, both the stereotypically masculine and the stereotypically feminine.

Granting God so-called feminine verbs has already to some extent succeeded, in that a medieval portrayal of God acting like a distant autocrat is nearly wholly absent from recent mainstream Christianity.

7. See, for example, Carl G. Jung, "Anima and Animus," in *Aspects of the Feminine*, trans. R. F. C. Hull (Princeton, N.J.: Princeton University Press, 1982), 95–100.

8. One such listing is in Anne Wilson Schaef, *Women's Reality: An Emerging Female System in a White Male World* (Minneapolis: Winston, 1981), 163.

9. See, for example, Sandra M. Schneiders, *Beyond Patching: Faith and Feminism in the Catholic Church* (New York: Paulist, 1991), 87–89.

Although God is still called Father, God is no longer described as a terrifying paterfamilias whose glance can kill, whose will determines one's fate. Any father in recent piety is more like an absent dad with little power and no authority. God is far more often the one who nurtures, forgives, feeds—stereotypically feminine action.

To attach actions like ruling and nurturing to gender, however, is pastorally problematic. No wholeness accrues to human persons when onesided exaggerations of behavior are assigned to one sex over the other. We have as yet no clarity about which human behaviors are tied to hormones, and in the absence of clarity, only stereotypes and prejudice guide our imagery. [10] Such cultural stereotypes gain more power to limit and determine human behavior once they have been rooted in the divine life. If God is nurturing and thus feminine, it is logical to assume that women are more nurturing than men, and this is hardly a model for interpersonal relationships and parental conduct that the church wishes to support. Some anthropological studies suggest that gender roles in primary societies assigned males the relatively simple tasks of planting or hunting and females the relatively complex tasks of creating culture, for example, turning grain into bread or making hides into clothing. [11]

Other feminist Christians, tending to minimize differences between women and men, are concerned that such labeling of divine behavior as masculine or feminine, male or female, will be ultimately counterproductive. While, like Aristotle, one may see sexual differences, learning from Aristotle's errors one must be exceedingly suspect of the judgments drawn from partial observations. Despite such patterns, distinctions do occur; should they be seen as descriptive or prescriptive? Praise that women are gloriously nurturing can limit a woman as much as scorn that women are merely nurturing. A recent study of ordained ministers, which set out to examine any differences between a feminine and a masculine style of ministry, discovered in fact no clear sex-based distinction; different styles of ministry depended on a wide variety of complex factors. [12] Gender is only one of many factors, and not nearly the sole determinative, in establishing individual behavior.

10. See Cynthia Fuchs Epstein, *Deceptive Distinctions: Sex, Gender, and the Social Order* (New Haven: Yale University Press, 1988), 232–40.

11. Tikva Frymer-Kensky, *In the Wake of the Goddesses: Women, Culture, and the Biblical Transformation of Pagan Myth* (New York: Free Press, 1992), 32–44.

12. Edward C. Lehman Jr., *Gender and Work: The Case of the Clergy* (Ithaca: State University of New York Press, 1993).

The theological dictum that "what is not assumed cannot be re-deemed" suggests that because in the incarnation God became human, neither exclusively male nor female, Christians are to downplay cultural expectations of gender as in any way constituting the human being before God. The church often must witness against cultural misogyny; for example, when in a Hindu society Protestants ordain women or when African Christians excommunicate those still practicing clitori-dectomy.[13] Minimizing feminist Christians are wary that cultural gender-based categories, which may be fallacious, still limit and devalue women's activity. One wonders whether the ordination of women in this century is responsible for or merely reflects the change from con-ceiving of the clergy as, like God, authorities, to, like God, caregivers. It may be that as God becomes devalued in an androcentric culture, there is less resistance to ascribing to God supposed feminine activity, since the activity of God is not deemed significant anyway.

Exactly these concerns encourage the church's liturgical language to avoid gender-specific nouns and to multiply divine verbs. A mother is undeniably a female image. However, to nurture, to guide, to feed, to embrace, to comfort, to midwife: these are not in any way explicitly gender-specific activities. Women do them, men do them, and some men do them better than some women. The Scriptures themselves contain hints of such breaking of gender stereotypes. It is Lady Wisdom who establishes justice in the city; it is the coming Messiah who will comfort the brokenhearted; it is Mary Magdalene who first preaches the resurrection. The kerygma intertwines masculine and feminine life into God and within the life of the Christian community.

Few verbs are absolutely tied to sexual function. Some of the bio-logically specific verbs the Christian tradition has refused to ascribe to God: *to ovulate, to ejaculate.* Other verbs, although biologically sug-gestive—*to birth, to bear, to nurse, to engender*—call up a range of meaning and an array of connotations that move God beyond gender. Prayers ought indeed to beg God to nurse this thirsty world. Happily, the verb *to nurse* evokes both a woman feeding her infant and a man caring for a dying companion. The verb is wider than the noun, a width God deserves.

13. Yusufu Nagaleni, personal conversation, April 29, 1993.

VERBS IN THE LITURGY

The liturgical assembly gathers around the verbs of God. That is, because God has acted and continues to act, the assembly responds with action. As Martin Luther said in his catechism, the Holy Spirit calls, gathers, enlightens, and sanctifies the church.[14] The assembly is that community called, gathered, enlightened, sanctified. The contemporary phenomenon known as seeker services, that is, Christian worship services focused on the outsider seeking religion, must always make clear the Christian theological assertion that all human search for God follows God's prior seeking for us. Even as the burgeoning adult catechumenate finds ways to ritualize a person's movement into the Christian community, Christians must remember that the church is not merely a volunteer association of like minds: without the initial action of God, the community would not exist.

For many centuries in its daily prayer, the church has framed the day with two biblical chants from Luke 1 that praise the actions of God. The appointed chant for the morning has been the Benedictus. Reminiscent of Jewish messianic hymns that employ warrior imagery,[15] the Benedictus invokes God's blessing for the battles of the coming day. The people sing together as soldiers requiring divine assistance, and they face their enemies in confidence, knowing that in the past God has looked favorably on them, redeemed them, raised them up, spoken to them, shown them mercy, remembered them, rescued them, enlightened them, guided them. Surely this God will also this day assist the faithful in their conflicts and terrors.

Yet each evening the church, setting aside its weapons, returns home to sing the Magnificat, the song of the serving maid. Before night the Christian is conscious of being alone before God: thus the poem begins in the singular. The day over, at nightfall the Christian knows that the poor have not yet been liberated, the battles for justice have not been successful. With the oppressed young woman, the petitioner recalls yet again the promise that God look favorably on the world,

14. Martin Luther, "The Small Catechism," in *The Book of Concord*, ed. Theodore G. Tappert (Philadelphia: Fortress, 1959), 345.

15. Raymond E. Brown, S.S., *The Birth of the Messiah: A Commentary on the Infancy Narratives in Matthew and Luke* (Garden City, N.Y.: Doubleday & Company, 1977), 378–92.

renew the strength of the faithful, scatter the proud, bring down the haughty, lift up the lowly, fill the hungry, dismiss the rich, help the faithful people.

The balance between the two poems demonstrates a biblical pattern of verbs. While the Maccabean soldier and the Galilean peasant offer two strikingly different metaphors for the human person, the poems do not distinguish divine action in any gender-specific way. Both poems begin in the confidence of the believer on whom God looks favorably. The poem of the warring man relies on God's tender mercy, the poem of the serving woman is confident that God will establish justice.

Many theologians have lamented that the church's concentration on the relationship of Jesus to God has left little space and time for focus on the Spirit. Yet, perhaps because the Spirit is not easily anthropomorphized, it is in descriptions of the Spirit where the church luxuriates in verbs. We see this, for example, in the two great medieval hymns invoking the Spirit. The "Veni Creator Spiritus," the ninth-century hymn by Rhabanus Maurus,[16] asks the Spirit to inspire, enlighten, anoint, impart, cheer, give peace, teach us God. The thirteenth-century hymn "Veni Sancte Spiritus,"[17] which became a proper chant for Pentecost Sunday, asks the Spirit to come, shine, fill the faithful, cleanse, refresh, heal, bend, melt, warm, guide, give. Whatever is in need meets the action of God's Spirit, an action always for life. God bends what is rigid, as if the Spirit were a masseuse kneading pain out of tight muscles, as if the Spirit were an archer preparing a bow from a bough. God cleanses what is filthy, as if the Holy Spirit were a washerwoman, scrubbing us and our soiled white garments on the washboard of the cross.

But it is not only in liturgical language that Christians praise God's verbs. The assembly enacts the verbs of God. The faithful people become the body of Christ; they do the actions of God. The liturgy is the school of faith, the place where one learns how to act like God. Thus baptism, inspired by the actions of the Spirit, washes what is dirty, drowns what is dying, clothes the naked, enlightens the dim-sighted,

---

16. One translation is by John Webster Grant, "O Holy Spirit, by Whose Breath," in *The Hymnal 1982* (New York: Church Hymnal Corporation, 1985), #501.

17. One translation is by Peter J. Scagnelli, "Holy Spirit, Lord Divine," in *Worship*, 3d ed. (Chicago: GIA Publications, 1986), #857.

anoints and embraces the newcomer. God's verbs become the verbs of the assembly, in hopes that, taught these actions in the liturgy, believers will enact such a lively God throughout their lives.

In sacramental life Christians model divine action. The stories of faith relate that God has fed the poor, provided wine for the sorrowing, gathered the isolated into community. In the eucharistic liturgy the church copies God's actions by serving bread and wine and by enlarging the circle of the faithful, again with the intent that, the liturgy over, Christians continue to enact God's verbs by feeding the hungry and embracing the lonely. The faithful praise God for keeping covenant with them, for loving them all the way to the cross; and so at marriages Christians attempt such divine action in their own lives, by promising to be faithful and to love until death. Christians praise God for caring for humans even past the boundary of death; and so at funerals Christians attempt such divine action themselves, by tending the corpse, by commending the dead to God and by trusting in the resurrection. In Martin Luther's version of the great processional litany of the medieval church, the believer begs God to rule, govern, guide, beat down, send, accompany, raise up, comfort, help, preserve, direct, guard, protect, heal, strengthen . . . : the list goes on.[18] Quite different from the "help us to realize" prayers, such a litany begs God to act in the world. Part of that action, but only part, will be to form believers into the body of Christ so that they become one of God's outstretched arms in the world. God's verbs dictate human actions.

When Christians in the United States reformed their liturgical language a generation ago, Protestants from Jacobean English and Roman Catholics from Latin, most published liturgical texts were marked by spare speech, simple syntax, sometimes even a childish vocabulary, as if the only alternative to archaic language was rudimentary speech. It is gratifying to see liturgical prayer moving away from those simplistic patterns into more enriched speech. Biblical images are inspiring more and richer verbs. God is asked not only to rule but to embrace. In spite of a tendency in contemporary speech for brevity, even terseness, Thomas Cranmer's superb sense of prayer language teaches the value of the doublet: two verbs placed side by side give the assembly time

18. "The Litany," in *Lutheran Book of Worship* (Minneapolis: Augsburg Publishing House, 1978), 168–73.

to pray, broaden the petition, illustrate that no single word is large enough, and invite the faithful to rest between the two words.[19] The classic Ash Wednesday collect, with its "hatest nothing and dost forgive . . . create and make . . . repenting and acknowledging," exemplifies this openness for every individual petitioner. Verbs large enough for the entire community's imagination and sentences with several verbs each will help move the prayer toward the depth that God is.

19. Daniel B. Stevick, *Language in Worship: Reflections in a Crisis* (New York: Seabury, 1970), 23–25.

eleven

CONTINUAL AND FAITHFUL REFORMATION

It is one thing to analyze the church's current liturgical language about God and to propose deletions, emendations, and additions. It is quite another thing to effect such changes. We do not even know where the churches presently stand on these convoluted issues. For how many Christians is God Zeus, or Superperson? How many assemblies are calling God Mother? Is the church's message of divine mercy being buried under the ruins of ancient temples, or have we instead fields where a thousand flowers bloom, many of which have their religious roots anywhere but in the Christian tradition? For some denominations, for some congregations, for some people, the greater danger is conserving liturgical tradition so carefully that the language of the faith suffocates in its glass case; for others, the danger comes from treating public worship as if it were the self-expression of the liturgists. In both cases, liturgical failure is not far away: religious language that never changes cannot breathe with the Spirit of God, and worship that is recast weekly cannot carry the prayers and praise of the faithful.

Church reforms must be respectful of the people's piety. Despite the rapid liturgical changes of our lifetime, the Sunday worshipers are not best understood as the guinea pigs for some liturgists' perpetual editing projects. Christians are baptized into a creed and, nurtured in a specific denomination and parish, grow into a certain style of prayer and praise. On a Sunday morning they can expect to rehearse the ritual that carries God to them. They can expect not to be manipulated by those who type up the services. The faithful are not like goslings following their Mother Goose, waddling along behind the presider. The liturgy is not to be conceived as primarily a vehicle for consciousness-raising, a way to force people to pray in the way the leaders wish they would.

Reforms must be rooted in the best of the Christian tradition. Human religion is an endlessly fascinating study, and the linguistic systems of other religions can be alluring. It is easier to invent a new religion or to appropriate bits and pieces from others that appear to meet current needs than it is to study one's own tradition: to hear the Bible speak the gospel of God's mercy, to learn the languages formative of one's faith, to join both classic and contemporary theologians in their struggle for meaning and expression, to cooperate with large groups of Christians toward new ways to proclaim the gospel. We need each others' visions: systematicians must acknowledge the inadequacy of the church's formulations, and impatient iconoclasts must study not only Hindu or Lakota tradition, but Christian as well. The Christian tradition has expressed the mercy of God in ways brilliant and vibrant although scarcely known, as well as in ways stupid and oppressive yet repeated every Sunday. The reforms must begin by discovering the healthiest roots and cultivating around them.

Yet the tendency of many people to keep God safely in their childhood, or perhaps in a medieval fantasy, means that liturgists, while respectful of the assembly's speech, must always be moving it forward: both the speech and the assembly. As the community grows and deepens, as each person matures, as the vernacular changes and metaphors alter their connotations, liturgical language continuously evolves. The newer speech will be different from several decades past, yet still remain the shared metaphor of the community. Those who teach and preach in the church must always be calling out for deeper, truer, more lively language for God. Studying the psalter is perhaps the best way to begin, by letting the Scriptures themselves model speech for God that is fanciful and undomesticated. Were the search for more faithful speech to mark the church, the speech itself would not be far behind. Christian formulations must change to stay the same; that is, the incarnation cries out for continual redactions of speech, for constant clarification, in order to articulate in a new time the message of God's mercy. Those Christians who return to the assembly after missing a decade or two of worship must expect that the language of the community, just like the speech of the culture, will have changed.

Paul Ricoeur comments that there are no living metaphors in the dictionary.[1] That is, metaphors tend to ossify, and it is largely moribund metaphors that constitute formal dictionary definitions. The language of the church must walk the balance beam: on one side are the innovative metaphors, words, and phrases that show God in tomorrow's light; and on the other side are doctrinal speech, formal definitions from the theological past, the entries in the Christian dictionary. Liturgical language, the weekly recitation of the words of the faithful, draws from these both and interweaves them, the creative phrases enlivening the creeds, the doctrine guiding the innovations. The challenge is weekly, never ceasing. Theologians can finally lay down their pens, saying with Gregory of Nyssa, "Since the Deity is too excellent and lofty to be expresssed in words, we have learned to honor in silence what transcends speech and thought."[2] But next Sunday comes another liturgy: the church cannot be silent. Worshipers assemble weekly, to pray the old and new metaphors, in a perpetually evolving yet always steadfast succession of words.

Fortunately the liturgy is not a seamless robe. Hymns are composed by the hundreds each year, sung by one parish or thousands, for one year or for centuries. Denominational committees clean their hymn collections every other decade, and the off-decades are marked by numerous publications of alternative hymnody. Hymnody is the best place for metaphoric experimentation. People can sing words they will not say. Yet the fact that congregational song provides an excellent opportunity for creativity does not mean that only hymns written last year should be sung. Part of the genius of hymnody is to connect present piety with past, to enrich the worshipers' metaphors with those they would not have thought of, to link present praise to the words and phrases of earlier centuries and distant saints.[3] But while conscientiously keeping alive the hymnic treasures of the church, parishes can experiment with new hymns. Some will be an open window through which

1. Paul Ricoeur, "Biblical Hermeneutics," in *Semeia* 4, ed. John Dominic Crossan (Missoula, Mont.: Scholars Press, 1975), 80.

2. Gregory of Nyssa, "Against Eunomius," in *A Select Library of Nicene and Post-Nicene Fathers*, ed. Philip Schaff and Henry Wace, 2d series (New York: Christian Literature Company, 1893), 5:147.

3. Gail Ramshaw, *Words That Sing* (Chicago: Liturgy Training Publications, 1992), 8.

the living Spirit of God blows into the stagnant air. Others will be just plain embarrassing, the poet whomping the assembly over the head with words too trivial or heretical ever to become the language of the faithful.

On the opposite end of the liturgical continuum are the creeds, the words at baptism, and the ecumenical historic texts. Caution is necessary in how these are changed, but that does not mean no change can occur. These English texts will and must change. No individual translation is sacrosanct. A continuing question is when or how often these texts are appointed for use. That the Nicene Creed's Christology "God from God, Light from Light" is relatively meaningless for many contemporary Americans means that one can chose whether to use the creed, and one can study its categories in adult classes. The church does not, however, authorize the presider to rewrite the Nicene Creed, expecting worshipers to affirm their faith in words they have never seen, words in every likelihood rather narrowly circumscribing the view of the contemporary author.

A range of liturgical texts exists between hymnody and the historic ecumenical pieces. The liturgy's prayers, whether the concise prayer-of-the-day or the intercessions, although spoken by one individual are communal liturgical speech. The weekly composed intercessions are a good vehicle for introducing new speech: yet often the intercessions are so marked by idiosyncratic syntax and personal reverie that they are no longer the prayers of the church, but a second homily by an enthusiastic poet. Just because a prayer has a single speaker does not mean it can be personally cast. In fact, the eucharistic prayer, best declaimed by a single presiding voice, carries the highest obligation to be the words of the assembly. Finally, despite popular notions that preachers can use the homily to tell their own story, sermons are also liturgical texts, instruction in the language of the faith, a rehearsal of the gospel in old and new words. The homily concludes with the people's "Amen" precisely because the people heard in the preacher's words their own faith.

The church must cultivate the Christian tree, weeding around its roots, pruning the tree so it bears edible fruit. At a recent high school graduation at a girls' school, an unchurched senior won a national prize for an essay in which she proposed a conversation between the Roman authors Horace and Catullus. When this emerging feminist comes to discover God, if she is to be engaged by the Christian church, the church's message must be cast in the speech of her contemporary experience: she will know the metaphors of the Greco-Roman world far better than the local pastor will. The church must find the words that articulate, not Jupiter or Artemis, but the triune God. The triune God is a deity intertwined with humankind, and the church's task is to discover how a God intertwined with human speech and categories finds expression in the liturgy.

In Martin Buber's collection of Hasidic legends is the following tale:

> After the maggid's death, his disciples came together and talked about the things he had done. When it was Rabbi Schneur Zalman's turn, he asked them, "Do you know why our master went to the pond every day at dawn and stayed there for a little while before coming home again?" They did not know why. Rabbi Zalman continued: "He was learning the song with which the frogs praise God. It takes a very long time to learn that song."[4]

So with the feminist reform of liturgical language: it will take a long time to learn the new song. The tasks are monumental. Here is a partial list: distinguish God from both Zeus and Superman; eliminate the pronoun *he* for God; adopt what is appropriate and discard what is not from other religions' vocabularies; make God's names and Christ's title gender-neutral; confront the myth of the crown; continue the work of the Cappadocians—why do we imagine trinitarian language took only three centuries to evolve?—so that the Trinity says mercy; attend to anthropomorphisms; enliven objective metaphors; and triple the verbs for God. We can concede that this will be a hundred-year project, but only if the church is zealously engaged in the endless and exacting tasks of reform today.

4. Martin Buber, *Tales of the Hasidim: The Early Masters* (New York: Schocken, 1947), 111.

BIBLIOGRAPHY

A work such as this arises in conversation with many others. Throughout this book, citations in notes have allowed the reader to trace specific references, but here a bibliography is provided that lists the current major studies in the various pertinent fields that have most significantly informed my thought.

Of the many studies that define and describe feminism, I found particularly helpful Carol Lee Bacchi, *Same Difference: Feminism and Sexual Difference* (Sydney: Allen & Unwin, 1990); Josephine Donovan, *Feminist Theory: The Intellectual Traditions of American Feminism* (New York: Ungar, 1986); Cynthia Fuchs Epstein, *Deceptive Distinctions: Sex, Gender, and the Social Order* (New Haven: Yale University Press, 1988); and Elizabeth H. Fox-Genovese, *Feminism without Illusions: A Critique of Individualism* (Chapel Hill: University of North Carolina Press, 1991).

Studies that discuss the androcentric nature of language include Dale Spender, *Man Made Language* (London: Routledge and Kegan Paul, 1980); Deborah Cameron, *Feminism and Linguistic Theory* (New York: St. Martin's Press, 1985); and Casey Miller and Kate Swift, *Words and Women: New Language in New Times*, 2d ed. (San Francisco: HarperCollins, 1991).

Studies that deal explicitly with feminism and religion, although in very different ways, are M. Esther Harding, *Woman's Mysteries: Ancient and Modern* (New York: Longmans Green 1935); the collection edited by Nancy Auer Falk and Rita M. Gross, *Unspoken Worlds: Women's Religious Lives* (Belmont, Calif.: Wadsworth, 1989); Ursula King, *Women and Spirituality: Voices of Protest and Promise* (New York: New Amsterdam, 1989); and Anne Carr and Elisabeth Schüssler Fiorenza, eds., *The Special Nature of Women? Concilium* 1991/6 (Philadelphia: Trinity Press International, 1991).

Several of the many historical studies that I found pertinent are Pamela Berger, *The Goddess Obscured: Transformation of the Grain Protectress from Goddess to Saint* (Boston: Beacon, 1985); Kari Elisabeth Børresen, ed., *Image of God and Gender Models in Judeo-Christian Tradition* (Oslo: Solum, 1991); Caroline Walker Bynum, *Jesus as Mother: Studies in the Spirituality of the High Middle Ages* (Berkeley: University of California

Press, 1982); Gerda Lerner, *The Creation of Patriarchy* (New York: Oxford, 1986); Carl Olson, ed., *The Book of the Goddess, Past and Present: An Introduction to Her Religion* (New York: Crossroad, 1985); and Marina Warner, *Alone of All Her Sex: The Myth and the Cult of the Virgin Mary* (New York: Knopf, 1976).

Works that deal with the broad questions of the feminist Christian language of faith and worship include: Rosemary Radford Ruether, *Sexism and God-Talk: Toward a Feminist Theology* (Boston: Beacon, 1983); Sallie McFague, *Models of God: Theology for an Ecological, Nuclear Age* (Philadelphia: Fortress, 1987); Marjorie Proctor-Smith, *In Her Own Rite: Constructing Feminist Liturgical Tradition* (Nashville: Abingdon, 1990); and Elizabeth A. Johnson, *She Who Is: The Mystery of God in Feminist Theological Discourse* (New York: Crossroad, 1992). Works on specific issues include Catherine Mowry LaCugna, *God for Us: The Trinity and Christian Life* (San Francisco: HarperCollins, 1991), and Ruth C. Duck, *Gender and the Name of God: The Trinitarian Baptismal Formula* (New York: Pilgrim, 1991).

Several of the many books that present feminist Christian worship resources are Rosemary Radford Ruether, *Women-Church: Theology and Practice of Feminist Liturgical Communities* (San Francisco: Harper & Row, 1985); Ruth Duck, *Dancing in the Universe: Hymns and Songs* (Chicago: GIA, 1992); Janet Morley, *All Desires Known*, rev. ed. (Ridgefield, Conn.: Morehouse, 1994); and Miriam Therese Winter, *Woman Prayer, Woman Song* (Oak Park, Ill.: Meyer-Stone, 1987).

Scholars who have articulated a feminist Christian theology include Anne E. Carr, *Transforming Grace: Christian Tradition and Women's Experience* (San Francisco: Harper & Row, 1988); Elisabeth Moltmann-Wendel, *A Land Flowing with Milk and Honey: Perspectives on Feminist Theology* (New York: Crossroad, 1986); Sandra M. Schneiders, *Beyond Patching: Faith and Feminism in the Catholic Church* (New York: Paulist, 1991); Elisabeth Schüssler Fiorenza, *In Memory of Her: A Feminist Theological Reconstruction of Christian Origins* (New York: Crossroad, 1984); Patricia Wilson-Kastner, *Faith, Feminism, and the Christ* (Philadelphia: Fortress, 1983); and Pamela Dickey Young, *Feminist Theology/Christian Theology: In Search of Method* (Minneapolis: Fortress, 1990).

Scholars who have examined biblical texts and their use in the tradition include: Elisabeth Schüssler Fiorenza, *But She Said: Feminist*

Practices of Biblical Interpretation (Boston: Beacon, 1992); Phyllis Trible, *God and the Rhetoric of Sexuality* (Philadelphia: Fortress, 1978); and Carol A. Newsom and Sharon H. Ringe, eds., *The Women's Bible Commentary* (Louisville: Westminster/John Knox Press, 1991).

Two examples of ecofeminism are Sallie McFague, *The Body of God: An Ecological Theology* (Minneapolis: Fortress, 1993), and Rosemary Radford Ruether, *Gaia and God: An Ecofeminist Theology of Earth Healing* (San Francisco: HarperCollins, 1992).

Womanist Christians who have contributed their African American perspective to the discussion of the language of faith include Kelly Delaine Brown, "Who Do They Say That I Am? A Critical Examination of the Black Christ," Ph.D. diss., Union Theological Seminary, 1988; Jacquelyn Grant, *White Women's Christ and Black Women's Jesus: Feminist Christology and Womanist Response* (Atlanta: Scholars Press, 1989); and Delores S. Williams, *Sisters in the Wilderness: The Challenge of Womanist God-Talk* (Maryknoll, N.Y.: Orbis, 1993).

Jewish women whose work is particularly instructive for Christian reflection include Tamar Frankel, *The Voice of Sarah: Feminine Spirituality and Traditional Judaism* (San Francisco: Harper & Row, 1990); Tikva Frymer-Kensky, *In the Wake of the Goddesses: Women, Culture, and the Biblical Transformation of Pagan Myth* (New York: Free Press, 1992); and Judith Plaskow, *Standing Again at Sinai: Judaism from a Feminist Perspective* (San Francisco: Harper & Row, 1990).

Christians who oppose feminist proposals are well represented in the eighteen essays in Alvin Kimel Jr., ed., *Speaking the Christian God: The Holy Trinity and the Challenge of Feminism* (Grand Rapids: Eerdmans, 1992). Other conservative arguments are found in Donald G. Bloesch, *The Battle for the Trinity: The Debate over Inclusive God-Language* (Ann Arbor: Servant Publications, 1985), and Susanne Heine, *Matriarchs, Goddesses, and Images of God: A Critique of a Feminist Theology*, trans. John Bowden (Minneapolis: Augsburg, 1989).

Several post-Christian feminists who articulate their current positions are Mary Daly, *Gyn/Ecology: The Metaphysics of Radical Feminism* (Boston: Beacon, 1978); Carol P. Christ, *Laughter of Aphrodite: Reflections on a Journey to the Goddess* (San Francisco: Harper & Row, 1987); and Daphne Hampson, *Theology and Feminism* (Oxford: Basil Blackwell, 1990).

Feminist ritual collections include Zsuzsanna E. Budapest, *The Holy Book of Women's Mysteries*, 2 vols. (Los Angeles: Susan B. Anthony Coven No. 1, 1979 and 1980); Starhawk, *The Spiral Dance: A Rebirth of the Ancient Religion of the Great Goddess* (San Francisco: Harper & Row, 1979); and Barbara G. Walker, *Women's Rituals: A Sourcebook* (San Francisco: Harper, 1990).

INDEX

NAME INDEX

Achtemeier, E., 96 n.8
Altman, N., 118 n.21
Andrews, E. and F., 118 n.19
Aquinas, Thomas, 16, 18, 24–25, 48, 90, 94–95, 112
Aristotle, 4, 10, 18, 79, 106, 123 n.5, 125
Augustine, 7, 17, 22, 81–83, 87–88
Baron, D., 23-24, 26
Barth, K., 18, 83
Beardsley, E., 27 n.11
Bendix, E., 26 n.10
Berger, B., 110
Berger, P., 12 n.10
Bevenour, J., 45 n.27
Bird, P., 19 n.30
Black Elk, 43
Borresen, K., 16 n.16
Braaten, C., 76 n.2
Bradley, R., 105 n.27
Brown, K. D., 54 n.9
Brown, R., 36 n.6, 37 n.8, 50 n.6, 127 n.15
Buber, M., 58 n.16, 135
Bultmann, R., 59
Burkert, W., 10 nn.2, 5, 78 n.10
Cady, S., 44 n.25
Calvin, J., 17
Cameron, D., 84 n.34
Campbell, J., 59
Catherine of Siena, 7, 89
Chadorow, N., 84 n.33
Chilton, B., 71 n.21
Christensen, T., 118 n.22
Clanton, J., 18 n.29
Clouser, R., 40 n.16
Collins, M., 71 n.20
Cook, R., 118 n.21
Corrington, G., 45 n.28
Cranmer, T., 129
Cross, F., 35 n.4
Curtis, E., 17 n.23

Cyril of Jerusalem, 115 n.13
D'Angelo, M., 78 n.9, 79 n.14
Dante Alighieri, 86, 89
Davidson, P., 102
Davies, J., 70 n.19
Day, J., 116 n.14
Denziger, H., 95 n.5
Dodd, C., 37 n.9, 72 n.22
Donne, J., 110
Donovan, J., 122 n.3
Dreyer, E., 104 n.23
Duck, R., 78 n.13, 90
Dunstan, S., 90, 102
Epstein, C., 125 n.10
Faulkner, W., 60
Fiorenza, E. S., 21 n.34, 76 n.4
Fortunatus, V., 117
Fox-Genovese, E., 83 n.30, 84 n.32
Franck, J., 14
Fraser, A., 101 n.11
Frye, N., 65 n.10
Frye, R., 96
Frymer-Kensky, T., 11 n.7, 125 n.11
Gerhardt, P., 77 n.6
Gertrud of Helfta, 112
Gibson, P., 58 n.15
Gilligan, C., 84 n.33
Grant, Jacquelyn, 40 n.15
Grant, John, 128
Gregory of Nazianzus, 19–20, 24
Gregory of Nyssa, 16, 133
Haugen, M., 118 n.20
Heber, R., 90
Henley, N., 32 n.24
Heschel, A., 121
Hill, W., 75 n.1, 83 n.28, 95 n.6
Hoekema, A., 16 n.16
Idle, C., 105 n.25
Jefferson, T., 40
Jenson, R., 39 n.11, 76 n.2
Jeremias, J., 78
Johnson, E., 28, 44 n.25, 76 n.1, 85 n.36, 95 n.6, 105 n.26

SUBJECT INDEX